DEADLINE POET

OR, MY LIFE AS A DOGGERELIST

CALVIN TRILLIN

WARNER BOOKS

A Time Warner Company

Warner Books Edition
Copyright © 1994 by Calvin Trillin
All rights reserved.

This Warner Books edition is published by arrangement with Farrar, Straus and Giroux, 19 Union Square West, New York, NY 10003.

Warner Books, Inc., 1271 Avenue of the Americas, New York, NY 10020

Ⓦ A Time Warner Company

Printed in the United States of America
First Warner Books Printing: June 1995
10 9 8 7 6 5 4 3 2 1

Library of Congress Cataloging-in-Publication Data
Trillin, Calvin.
    Deadline poet, or, My life as a doggerelist / Calvin Trillin. —
Warner Books ed.
    p.   cm
    ISBN 0-446-67130-4
    1. Trillin, Calvin—Authorship. 2. Poetry—Authorship.
3. Poetics.   I. Title. II. Title: Deadline poet. III. Title: My life
as a doggerelist.
[PS3570.R5Z465 1995]
811' .54—dc20   94-46653
                                                            CIP

Cover photograph by Michael McLaughlin

In Memory of

Emanuel P. Popolizio—Uncle Wally

DEADLINE
POET

1. *Inspiration*

Could there be anyone else who was inspired to write poetry by the presence of John Sununu? It has occurred to me that if I ever get to poets' heaven—as I envision it, it's a place where the accent is on any syllable you want it to be on and there are plenty of rhymes for "orange"—I might find myself feeling rather awkward during a discussion that turns toward how all of us poets acquired the vital spark of inspiration. In poets' heaven, that sort of thing would be the equivalent of telling war stories. This being a variety of paradise, other people would be genuinely interested in your war stories: as you spoke, the other poets would stare at you intently, while sipping nectar from flip-top cans that never run dry. William Shakespeare might talk passionately, if rather enigmatically, about how inspiring the Dark Lady of his sonnets was, and some of the other fellows would mention, say, a particularly breathtaking sunset or a monarch who, at just one remarkable moment in history, had the capacity to energize an entire people. Sooner or later, the other poets would look my way and I'd say, "Well, when George Bush was President of the United States, he had this guy from New Hampshire as chief of staff . . ."

Considering the type of poetry I do—I have heard it described as "verse of a light but nasty nature"—I should make it clear that the inspiration Sununu presented to me did not come entirely from his being a juicy target. It is true that I wrote my first weekly poem for *The Nation* in the summer of 1990, when he was the premier punching bag for those of us who are in the business of making snide and underhanded and generally unfair remarks about hardworking public officials. It is also true that at that time there happened to be a shortage of suitable punching bags. During most of the time that I'd been writing a column regularly—first for *The Nation* and then for a newspaper syndicate— I had been blessed with the consistently entertaining courtiers of the Reagan Administration. For people in my line of work, those were the glory days—the days when you opened your morning paper half expecting to read that the President had mistaken the White House caterer for the Chief of Naval Operations or that the Administration had attacked the deficit problem by inviting in a man who, while costumed rather persuasively as Cath-

erine of Aragon, stuck pins in an effigy of the national debt.

By the time I began my career in poetry, though,
the small-joke trade was trying to cope with what
you might call a serious gray-out. A year before this,
when Bush had been in office for only six months,
James G. Watt, Ronald Reagan's Secretary of the
Interior, returned to Washington and the evening
news—he dropped by a congressional committee
hearing to acknowledge, rather cheerfully, that he
had received $400,000 from a developer for making
a few calls to some old cronies at the Department
of Housing and Urban Development—and I had
found myself almost pathetically grateful to see him.

"We've missed you, Watt," I said to the figure
on my television screen. "We've missed those days
when you used to get down on your knees and pray
for Divine guidance in facing the decision on
whether to turn Yosemite over to Exxon or Mobil.
We've missed that cowboy hat you used to wear on
inspection trips out West—the one that made you
look like a regional auditor taking in the Calgary
Stampede. Welcome back, Watt!"

At that moment, I couldn't have named George
Bush's Secretary of the Interior. I was not alone in
my ignorance. Six months into most Administrations, the average citizen has long forgotten the
names of such public officials as the Secretary of
the Interior and the Secretary of Housing and Urban Development and the Secretary of Agriculture.

But in the Reagan Administration, it was the President who couldn't seem to recall the names of his cabinet secretaries. The rest of us had no trouble at all remembering them. Who could ever forget Ed Meese? As I watched Watt finish off his story of casual influence peddling, I realized how much I missed the entire Administration of Ronald Reagan. As my Army buddy Charlie might put it, those guys were a hoot.

I had known at the time that we would never again see the likes of, say, Alexander Haig. When Alexander Maximus left, I acknowledged in a column that what had flashed before my eyes was the final scene in *Shane*. Haig, on a white horse, is riding slowly out of town, his toga almost touching the dusty trail. I'm behind him on foot, in the Brandon de Wilde role. I'm shouting, "Haig! Haig! Please don't go, Haig! We need you, Haig! Come back, Haig!"

In the Reagan Administration, even subcabinet appointments could provide grist for our nasty little mills. In nostalgic moments, I sometimes thought of William Clark, who in his confirmation hearing for Deputy Secretary of State couldn't name the Prime Minister of South Africa and didn't seem dead certain of where England was. In 1990, a year and a half after all the Reagan people had gone back to their California country clubs, William Clark was still in my mind. I envisioned him wandering around the San Fernando Valley, under the impression he was in Belgium.

I thought of William Clark because there wasn't much in the Bush Administration to think about. It was gray in color. It was homogeneous. The President and all four members of what is sometimes known as the inner cabinet—the Secretaries of State, Defense, and the Treasury, plus the Attorney General—had attended either Yale or Princeton. (Dick Cheney, who left Yale after a year, finished up at the University of Wyoming, an experience that failed to turn him into a cowboy.) If there had been a hangout then for small-joke jackals of the press—some out-of-the-way beer joint with service so terrible that an observant customer could get a column out of it now and then—I would have pictured it full of long faces:

Russell is staring glumly into his beer, dispirited by an all-day attempt to find something funny or even faintly unusual about Samuel K. Skinner, then Secretary of Transportation, or Edward Madigan, the Secretary of Agriculture. "We are sculptors without clay," Russell finally says. "Or some similarly appropriate metaphor."

"Life has become an American Bankers Association convention," Art says. "We're sitting through the symposium on long-term debentures, and we can't get out. There's a metaphor for you, Russell."

At the end of the bar, an editorial cartoonist named Doug is complaining that the Bush people all look alike—all of them with the regular features of the father in the Dick and Jane readers. "Regular features," he says bitterly. "Jesus, I hate regular features!" In a cartoon Doug just handed in, his depiction of Nicholas Brady, the Secretary of the Treasury, was taken for Dick Thornburgh by the editorial-page editor, who demanded to know what the Attorney General was doing in a cartoon about the trade imbalance.

"I can't get over the President announcing that he won't eat broccoli," Dave says, shaking his head at the thought. "That's their idea of dash, not eating broccoli: 'How did things go at work today, dear?' 'I met a man who won't touch lima beans.' 'My, how colorful! What a character! You must bring him home to dinner sometime.' "

"Cheer up, guys," the bartender says, as he brings another round. "Don't forget: you've got Quayle."

The response is a wall of sullen stares. It has always made us even gloomier to be told that we have Quayle. It puts us in the position of some well-born but impecunious WASP who can't get any sympathy for his cash-flow problems because everyone takes it for granted that he has a trust fund.

Because we don't have Quayle. We never really had Quayle. Even as he was elected, in 1988, I wrote a column saying that Quayle wouldn't be of any use to us, since Quayle jokes were already at the level of knock-knock jokes. Telling jokes about Quayle, I said, was like telling jokes about Vanna White or Howard Cosell, the only difference being that those two citizens do not happen to be in the line of succession to the presidency. How, I lamented, could we expect to be paid for telling the same jokes that bartenders were handing out free with the peanuts and kids were bringing home from school? (At that time, some readers thought that remark about the kids bringing Quayle jokes home from school was an exaggeration—our crowd, I should say, often uses exaggeration for effect—but by May 14, 1992, *The New York Times* ran an item that began, "Even in the schoolyard, the adult world of the White House is a favorite target of ridicule, with the Vice President the butt of many jokes.")

No, we didn't have Quayle. All we had, in fact, was Sununu. If there was going to be only one punching bag available, I must admit, he was close to perfect. He had all the attributes we look for— arrogance, self-importance, and a management style that he might have picked up intact from the Emperor Caligula. Not since the relatively brief appearance several years before of Robert Bork— who turned out to be more interested in showing himself to be the smartest man in the room than he was in being on the Supreme Court—had Washington served up a character so intent on letting everybody know how intelligent he was. Sununu even *looked* something like a punching bag, much to the delight of political cartoonists who had become dispirited by the difficulty of telling all the Bush people apart.

Was I inspired by all of this? Yes, of course. But to poetry? Not exactly. What led me to poetry was that wondrously euphonious name—Sununu. I couldn't get his name out of my mind. "Sununu," I would murmur to myself, while riding the subway or doing some little task around the house, "Sununu." Sooner or later, the murmuring stretched out to "So *nu,* Sununu?" At some point, it became "If You Knew What Sununu." To me, that sounded like the title of a poem.

IF YOU KNEW WHAT SUNUNU

If you knew what Sununu
Knows about quantum physics and Greek
And oil explorations and most favored nations
And the secret handshake of Deke,

Maybe you, too, like Sununu,
Would adopt as your principal rule
That you are the brightest, you're lit the
    lightest,
And everyone else is a fool.

With the IQ that Sununu
Relentlessly tells us is his,
You might think you're paid to devote half
    your day to
Displaying yourself as a whiz.

But

If it's true that Sununu's
So smart, you'd think that he'd know
What always defines the truly fine minds:
The smartest guys don't let it show.

2. First Ladies

Four or five days after I submitted "If You Knew What Sununu" to *The Nation* as my first poem, it began to dawn on me that I couldn't write a poem about Sununu every week. I started looking around for what I suppose you'd have to call alternate punching bags. Given the fact that the public is much more interested in the life of the President than in his policies, the logical place to look for subjects was George Bush's family. In prose, I had commented on presidential families at least as far back as the Trumans. In discussing the familiarity with Harry Truman that people in my hometown affected while I was growing up, I observed that if everyone who claimed to have bought a necktie from Truman's haberdashery on Twelfth Street really had bought a necktie, the business would have been a phenomenal success and Clifton Daniel would now be married to the daughter of the Cravat

King of Kansas City. I hadn't been above making fun of Trish Nixon's recipe for Chicken Divan, in which the preparer pours two cans of chicken soup on some poor bird that is already a chicken. I had made sport of Jimmy Carter's siblings, and may have passed a churlish remark or two about his wife and children. I take considerable comfort from the fact that Carter, a committed Christian, must have forgiven me for that long ago—about the time I got around to forgiving him for Bert Lance.

But here I had a problem: not long after George Bush assumed the presidency, I had finally faced up to the troubling fact that I sort of liked Barbara Bush. Again, the comparison with the Reagan Administration was distressing. Nancy Reagan had been for me what the Red Menace used to be for J. Edgar Hoover: I sometimes felt that if she hadn't existed I would have had to make her up. In my column, I had broken a story out of Chicago that she had been called Bubbles in high school. I had talked about her obsession with high-fashion clothes—"loaned" by expensive designers in the way you might loan a quietly passed fifty-dollar bill to a customs inspector who looked like the sort of person who appreciated small favors. Speaking of the Reagans' thoughtfulness in not inflicting their children on us—or on themselves—I had reported a rumor that a photographer trailing Ronald Reagan, Jr., down Fifth Avenue observed him waving and yelling "Hiya, Dad!" to a man who turned out to be Joel McCrea.

Years after Nancy Reagan and her husband left the White House to live quietly in the Pacific Palisades house that those nice friends in California had bought for them, she was still providing copy for the small-joke trade—most notably with the publication of the book on her by sleazographer Kitty Kelley:

A SHORT REVIEW OF KITTY KELLEY'S BIOGRAPHY OF NANCY REAGAN

Oh, Kitty K., what hast thou wrought?
The dirt that in thy net thou'st caught
Must make the Reagans so distraught.
To know that Nancy's bad we ought.
This book, though, hath a bombshell brought:
She's even badder than we thought.

The book dished out dirt so indiscriminately— Mrs. R. was accused of smoking dope and having a dalliance with Frank Sinatra in the White House, not to speak of the run-of-the-mill lying and backstabbing we've come to expect from our public figures as revealed in biographies—that some readers must have found themselves feeling sympathetic toward its subject. Well, almost. To my mind, the prize anecdote of the book, illustrating the twin charms of complete coldness toward children and overpowering stinginess, reported that Mrs. Reagan often used presents brought to the White House to fulfill her own gift obligations—a habit that re-

sulted in one of the President's grandchildren having received for his birthday a stuffed animal that
he himself had inadvertently left at the White
House not long before, during one of his family's
ever so rare appearances there.

JUDGING NANCY

*You think she really did some things untoward
With Frankie S., the Chairman of the Board?
So what! The world is surely in a muddle
When two old folks can't have a little cuddle
Right after lunch, no matter where they are—
The White House or a small romantic bar.
And frankly, I don't really see the point
Of fainting at the thought she smoked a joint.
Oh sure, she lied, she stole, she slipped her
     shiv
Into some backs. All this I could forgive.
But one thing boggles even now my mind:
The teddy bear her grandson left behind.
Unrecognized, old* Ursus theodore
*Was tossed among the presents that this
     schnorrer
Reused. A birthday? Reach into the sack:
The little fellow gets his own bear back.
I do not judge our Nancy, like some folks.
I've crimes myself: harsh thoughts, bad jokes.
But when she meets her Maker, is she ready
To justify her treatment of that teddy?*

As the time came to lob some rotten tomatoes Mrs. Bush's way, I'd pick one up and turn it over in my hand for a while, like a pitcher waiting for a signal he likes. But I couldn't bring myself to throw it. The good fairy on my shoulder—the tiny creature I thought I had rid myself of long ago by making a sudden flicking motion toward an open microwave oven—kept saying, "Why would you want to bother a nice lady like that?" Nice lady? Yes, that was the phrase that came to mind when I thought about Barbara Bush. She seemed to be a nice lady. I realize that "nice lady" is considered an old-fashioned phrase, but Mrs. Bush is sort of old-fashioned herself. That's one of the things I like about her.

Which is all to say that a year and a half after George Bush was inaugurated, Mrs. Bush was still being given an easement in my column—and that easement transferred easily to my weekly verse. In fact, one of my first poems for *The Nation* was a two-stanza tribute to her:

FIRST LADY

I

We're grateful for the Premier Spouse we've
  got.
We value her for all the things she's not.
We're pleased she doesn't seem to be obsessed
With how her hair is done and how she's
  dressed.

Her visits with her kids (and with her spaniel)
Seem more than show, and more than
  semiannual.
Regarding those whose greed and glitzy ways
Remind historians of Rome's last days,
She knows the sort of trough in which one
  doesn't wallow.

II
It always helps to have an easy act to follow.

3. Son of Poet

You might say that I come from a poetic background: my father owned a restaurant for a while in Kansas City, and he used to write a couplet every day for the lunch menu. Most of his couplets were about pie—"Don't sigh / Eat pie" (his shortest), for instance, or "Let's go, warden, I'm ready to fry / My last request was Mrs. Trillin's pie" or "Mrs. Trillin's pie, so nutritious and delicious / Will make a wild man mild and a mild man vicious."

Although the sons of poets have historically been less likely than the sons of, say, musicians or organized-crime figures to go into their father's line of work, I found myself slipping into verse with fair regularity. For many years, I was basically a special-occasion poet. I specialized in epics. It was common for me to toss off a hundred lines or so for a wedding or a major anniversary. I still do that now and then. A lengthy effort for a friend in television news, for instance, included this heartfelt description of what they would call at the network awards banquets a broadcast journalist learning his craft:

> *He did the things that make fine newsmen*
> *   finer:*
> *Resculpt the hair, use just a touch of liner,*
> *Resolve that he would learn, by hook or crook,*
> *To cultivate a slightly vacant look.*

For a farewell dinner at the New York Public Library, I did a 100-liner that included this description of the library in its darkest hours, just before the renaissance that took place in the eighties:

> *Truth seekers went to find what they were*
> *   seeking.*
> *They found instead the roof above them*
> *   leaking.*
> *They found collections crumbled, tables pitted.*
> *They found on Thursdays they were not*
> *   admitted.*
> *In reading rooms they found such sad decay*
> *At one point even flashers stayed away.*

For one brief period in my early twenties, I confess, I wrote limericks—a form that is considered less than exalted even among special-occasion versifiers. The summer after I graduated from college, I was hired by Time Inc. to put together a booklet of thumbnail biographies describing the business leaders Time had invited from around the world to attend something called the International Industrial Development Conference. In the weeks before the conference, I got bored with listing directorships and degrees, and I found myself experimenting with limericks that had opening lines like "From Burma there came U Tin U, / Whom alphabetizers did rue." I remember only one of the limericks in its entirety:

> From Italy came Olivetti,
> Who, while eating his Apple Brown Betty,
> Scratched his bald head and ruefully said,
> "Why is it that everyone who has ever
>   written a poem about me finds it of such
>   extraordinary interest that my name
>   happens to rhyme with spaghetti?"

Yes, Apple Brown Betty was a regular dessert on the menu of my father's restaurant. No, from what I can remember, he never wrote a poem about it. No, I did not continue to write limericks, about desserts or anything else. By the time the conference actually took place, I had begun to occupy myself with one of my epics, and I read it aloud on the last evening: "Ode to Combined Assets of Thirty Billion and Other Holdings."

Just after the conference, I lived for a while in a London bed-sit, where I composed a poem on the subject of my landlady, Mrs. Krupevich, who, as far as I was able to tell, had no first language:

> *There lived a landlady on Collingham Place,*
> *And she had an accent that was hard to trace.*
> *She spoke bits of Polish, of English, of Greek.*
> *But bits of them all was all she could speak.*

Those lines could be sung as the lyrics to an old folk song, "Sweet Betsy from Pike," so my London landlady might have been the start of an interest in lyric writing that has taken me to the heights of the movie musicals our family used to shoot every summer in Nova Scotia, when our children were at the age of being willing to sing on camera. It was I who wrote the lyrics to the title song of one of the movies, a smoked-salmon mystery called *If There's No Nova Scotia in Nova Scotia, There Can't Be Any French Fries in France.*

But the core of my poesy (a word that I never thought I'd be able to use in reference to myself) remained special-occasion verse—for a daughter's high school graduation ("Her smile could sell / *La Tour Eiffel*") or an important birthday. On my wife's fiftieth, I wrote a poem called "An Explanation to Someone Who Finds It Hard to Believe That Alice Could Be Fifty." The first verse goes:

> *"No way," you say.*
> *"It simply cannot be.*
> *I would have guessed*

That barmen often ask her for I.D."
I know, I know.
She has that youthful glow
That still gives young men vapors.
She's fifty, though; I've seen her papers.

In other words, I had, at a rather advanced age, begun to write love poems. Not long after that, with John Sununu's name dancing through my head, I spoke to the editor of *The Nation*, the wily and parsimonious Victor S. Navasky, about the possibility of writing some light verse now and then on the events of the day. Navasky said he thought it would work best as a weekly offering. Just as easily as that, I became a deadline poet.

4. Career Opportunities
in Poetry

When I was in college, I took a writing course that required each student to turn in a one-page vignette every day of the week, except Saturday and Sunday. It was common for a student's confidence to swell as he tossed off the first week's worth of stories—as I remember, we didn't hear an instructor's opinion of our work until a couple of weeks had passed—and then, on about Tuesday or Wednesday of the second week, to roll a piece of blank paper in the typewriter and come to the sudden and devastating realization that seven one-page vignettes had used up his life experience.

I can imagine poets having similar difficulties. Sometimes I envision Wordsworth pacing around the house, growling at the wife and kids, as he tries in vain to think of a subject for his next poem.

"Why don't you just go for a walk, Bill," Mrs.

Wordsworth says. "Maybe you'll have intimations of immortality."

"I already had intimations of immortality, when I was a child," Wordsworth says. "Nobody writes two poems about intimations of immortality, woman."

Poets who are down a bit from Wordsworth on the poetry chain—poets who celebrate concrete events—don't face that sort of problem when it comes to inspiration. For my father, for instance, another day brought another kind of pie. It may well have been that on days when he had been thinking that he could simply never come up with another rhyme for "pecan," the baker produced rhubarb or a specialty of the house called black-bottom—an obvious rhyme with "got 'em."

The most easily inspired type of poets are, of course, cowboy poets. A lame heifer or a pot of burnt coffee is enough to set them off. While other poets are wandering around suffering from a short-age of inspiration, hoping to find a metaphor around the next corner, a cowboy poet will be turning out a sixty-liner on, say, a horse named Flag ("You'd take him for a humble nag . . ."). The only cowboy poet I've met—Baxter Black, who is also a veterinarian—was once inspired by the laundry that accumulated during the day at his veterinary clinic. The resulting poem could, I believe, be summed up by a thoughtful poetry critic as "not for the fainthearted."

I met Baxter, who has been called "the premier

cowboy poet of the West," at a booksellers' meeting in Denver, where he was pushing his latest book of poetry, *Croutons on a Cow Pie*. I felt an immediate kinship with him—partly, I think, because, choosing among all his impressive reviews, Baxter had decided to put on the back of that book a single quotation that I identified with. A line from the *Des Moines Register*, it said, in the unadorned prose traditionally favored on the range, "Baxter Black is not your normal poet."

Baxter Black is only one among dozens (or maybe hundreds) of cowboy poets—enough to people official cowboy poetry gatherings in any number of Western states. It has always seemed remarkable to me that cowboys—people whose duties require little in "communications skills," people who prize taciturnity, people who traditionally have a suspicion of what cowboys in the movies always call "book larnin' "—are the only American occupational group to have created a genre of poetry.

Of course, there have been American poets who were strongly identified with some non-poetic calling. William Carlos Williams, for instance, was a doctor. But his poetry was neither for doctors nor about doctoring. If Williams had been a doctor poet in the way that Baxter Black and his pardners are cowboy poets, he would have written couplets like "Why, that old doc had to climb up on a tall ladder / Just to check the swelling in that lady's gallbladder." (Cowboy poets find precise meter about as useful as an English saddle.) Wallace Stevens was for many years an insurance executive, but, as far as I know, he didn't write any sonnets about how a company that managed to sneak an exception for rising water into homeowners' policies could often wriggle out of paying off on hurricane damage.

There isn't any insurance-executive poetry or washing-machine-servicemen poetry or even professors-of-comparative-literature poetry. There are no dentist poets, which is a pity. I could just about guarantee that my own dentist—a healer we usually refer to as Sweeney Todd, D.D.S.—would leap at the opportunity to knock off a few stanzas, if the money were right. As the dental equivalent of a cowboy poet, Sweeney might write:

> *The cavities stretch out before him*
> *From morn to the end of the day.*
> *But he takes up his drill like a carbine—*
> *He's a soldier who's fighting decay.*
> *The enemy—plaque—presses onward,*
> *And tosses our man for a loss.*
> *But he rallies the troops with his war cry:*
> *"Remember: you simply must floss."*

I can easily imagine barber poetry ("Because he didn't get a tip, he / Made sure the count looked like a hippie") and deli-owner poetry ("He has a yacht, he has a castle and a plane. The man's in clover / And all from six words at the scale: Okay if it's a little over?"). I can imagine limos triple-parked in front of the Regency Hotel on Park Avenue to whisk bards away to their appointed finagling at the conclusion of the public reading that traditionally closed the annual gathering of investment-banker poets. Inside, the dining room is hushed as an arbitrageur reads:

He always bought the day before the rise.
He always sold the day before the dive.
We never knew the secret of his touch.
But now we know. He's doing two to five.

What surprises me about the absence of other occupational specialties in the field now totally dominated by cowboy poetry is that there seems to be money in this. If I were asked to name a couple of poets who make a nice steady living off their poetry, the names that would come to mind are Yevgeny Yevtushenko and Baxter Black. In general, poets are not notable for their incomes. At the high-school career-day fair, you don't see a large crowd around a booth touting opportunities in poetry. Why? Because the brochure handed out there would say something like

OPPORTUNITIES IN POETRY

Most poems aren't in magazines at all.
You see them scrawled in pencil on a stall.
A poet must feel grateful writing for
Most any place where MEN's *not on the door—*

Especially any place that pays a fee
That varies just a tiny bit from free.

Naturally, I thought about this as I was about to begin negotiations with the wily and parsimonious Victor S. Navasky. Although *The Nation* prides itself on defending the interests of downtrodden classes throughout the world, Navasky has always been willing to make an exception for writers.

His offer was simple. He would pay me the same for each poem as he had once paid me for each column. I have previously corrected the widespread misapprehension that what I received from *The Nation* for each column was what Navasky had originally offered—"something in the high two figures." As I reported in a book called *With All Disrespect*, I turned the matter over to my high-powered literary agent, Robert "Slowly" Lescher, and instructed him to play hardball. Slowly got Navasky up to a hundred dollars.

Although Navasky didn't say exactly how he reached the figure of a hundred dollars a poem— what I believe poets call a century—I do recall that after he took a look at the Sununu poem he called me on the telephone and said, "How long does it take you to write one of these?"

"I usually write them on Sunday," I said. "Which is at least time and a half, and in most trades double time. There is also the matter of poetic inspiration—walking on the windswept bluff, and all that.

Just to get from here to a windswept bluff that could be considered remotely inspirational . . ."

As I said that, I could hear his calculator clicking away. "How about a hundred?" he said.

What I realized instantly—what I suppose he meant me to realize instantly—was that I would be getting the same money for a poem as for an 1,100-word column.

"What are the conditions?" I asked. With the wily and parsimonious Victor S. Navasky, there is always a condition or two.

"Don't tell any of the real poets you're getting that much," he said.

"Your secret is safe with me," I assured him.

At first I didn't think a century sounded like much, compared to the sort of loot that I could imagine Yevtushenko and Baxter Black pulling in. But then I learned that poets are normally paid by the line. Three-fifty or four dollars a line is fairly common, I was told, and ten dollars a line is probably tops. Since I was being paid by the poem, I realized, all I had to do to become the highest-paid poet in the world—someone whose per-line rate was five times higher than anyone else's—was to write a two-line poem. The opportunity soon presented itself, when the reunification of Germany brought celebration that was just short of universal:

GERMAN REUNIFICATION: THE DOWNSIDE

Here's the fate that could befall us:
Deutschland, Deutschland, über alles.

For the first time, I could empathize with Philip J. Rooney, of Waste Management Inc. In a column a couple of years before, I had mentioned him as someone who, by pulling down a salary of $14,276,000, finished at the top of *Business Week*'s annual survey of executive compensation. At the time, I'd assumed that Rooney and I had little in common professionally, beyond the fact that in my youth waste management was a field in which fathers occasionally suggested that their sons might find career opportunities ("If you don't straighten out, you're going to find yourself on the back of a garbage truck"). After the poem on German reunification, though, I understood that once that *Business Week* survey was published Philip J. Rooney must have marched off to manage waste every morning with a song on his lips, and not simply because of what $14,276,000 can buy. He must have been imbued with the gratifying feeling you get from working for the absolute top dollar in your field—a feeling available to me anytime I decided to write a two-line poem. The fact that the person paying me at that gloriously premium rate was the wily and parsimonious Victor S. Navasky made the moment even sweeter.

I found writing two-line poems a shot in the arm even if the subject of the poem was rather grim—the incident, for instance, in which the twenty-seven police officers who surrounded Rodney King after a high-speed car chase in Los Angeles could think of no way to get him handcuffed and into the back of a police cruiser except to beat him with nightsticks and kick him for a while:

THE PICKED UP BY THE LOS ANGELES POLICE DEPARTMENT BLUES

If I done right or I done wrong,
I'd sooner be held by the Vietcong.

The world had its problems, but at least I was, in a manner of speaking, raking it in. I have never stopped getting a thrill out of writing one of my fifty-dollar-a-line specials—even when, as in the case of Madonna, the subject was raking in quite a bit more than I was:

ON THE PUBLICATION OF *Sex*, BY MADONNA

Madonna has unusual friends.
Her book consists of odds—and ends.

5. *Summer in the Deadline Poetry Game*

Summer, the season of my inauguration as a deadline poet, is normally a quiet time for jackals of the press. Except during an election year, politicians and government officials slow down to the point at which, as the saying goes, they can't do a whole lot of harm. People continue to kill each other in a variety of wars around the world—some foreign countries, after all, have seasons that don't correspond to ours—but we don't get as exercised about it. As a deadline poet in the summer, I didn't even have a weekly deadline: as I pointed out in one of my hundred-dollar columns many years ago, *The Nation* publishes only every other week in July and August, even though the downtrodden are oppressed every single day of the year. In the summer, with the slower pace of events, a deadline poet's thoughts are likely to turn away from government and politics to, say, culture:

CHANGE OF SEASONS

New movies, which are mostly dumb, are in
*   the summer*
Even dumber.

The summer's when I feel most like an ancient
*   fogy,*
Missing Bogey.

I'm grateful when fall's cooling breezes come.
Back to dumb.

Or to science:

TRUE LOVE

The newest research shows
(So says the Times, *in Section C)*
That birds and bees and beasts
Are more promiscuous than we.

The birds we always thought
Were faithful till the day they died
Are almost sure to have
A little something on the side.

The California mouse
So far's the only thing they've found
That's married, you might say:
This mouse just doesn't play around.

Yes, California mice
Have just one lifelong love to give.
It's odd they stay so true,
Especially living where they live.

During that first summer of deadline poetry, though, so much news erupted that some jackals of the press were forced to scurry back into town from their dark little lairs. In July, Justice William Brennan had resigned from the Supreme Court, and President Bush announced that he was nominating David Souter, of New Hampshire, to fill the vacancy. Instantly the jackals of the press and any number of pressure groups brought up their big research artillery; you could almost hear the rumble of the Nexis checks. The life of David Souter was revealed—an operation that one jackal described to me as "like opening the door to an empty room."

Souter was as close as a Federal Appeals Court judge could get to being a man without a record. He hadn't had enough time on the federal bench to write any significant decisions. He was not someone who had in his youth dashed off law-review articles that could be mined for embarrassing weirdness. A bachelor, he had no indiscreet wife or drug-addled children. Like someone who had just been named, say, Foreign Minister of the People's Republic of China, Souter became the subject of conversations that were short on facts but long on analysis. In some circles, grist for an entire dinner-party conversation could be provided by a newspaper report that, say, Souter had long been in the habit of picking up a neighbor—an elderly woman—every Sunday morning and driving her to church:

"Church every Sunday? How do you think he'll be on separation of church and state?"

"That's not the point. The point is that he's not really a recluse who has no contact with ordinary people: he probably has a nice chat with that old woman every Sunday. Keeps in touch."

"I wonder if the old dear has ever had an abortion."

"He can't be anti-abortion. It's an Episcopalian church. There's no such thing as an Episcopalian who's anti-abortion."

"George Bush is an Episcopalian who's anti-abortion."

For the groups that had to decide whether to make an all-out push against almost any nominee from the Bush White House, a man with no record did not present a tempting target. But they were concerned—if for no other reason than what was being written about John Sununu's having assured conservatives that Souter could be counted on to help overturn *Roe v. Wade*. Sununu turned out to be wrong about that—his tendency to be arrogant about being right when he was, in fact, wrong, was always part of what endeared him to the small-joke crowd—but in the summer of 1990 it was difficult for a Democratic senator on the Judiciary Committee to know:

QUESTIONING DAVID SOUTER
(Three Tacks Democratic Senators Could Take)

UNFOCUSED RELUCTANCE
I'll grant you it's no smoking gun.
In some ways, though, it's hotter:
Can we confirm a judge who's got
Sununu's imprimatur?

SIMPLE WONDER
A character beyond dispute?
No accusations to refute?
Did no one ever institute
A suit that claimed you took some loot?
Not once, did you go on a toot?
Or hit some brute right in the snoot
When he, attempting to be cute,
Insisted that a man named Sout-
er would, of course, be known as Zoot?
Or taste . . . er . . . ah . . . forbidden fruit?
Or once neglect your paper route?

MEASURED RELIEF
The others mentioned being mainly loonies,
I'll settle for a no one from the boonies.

The hearings, of course, wouldn't take place until fall. Until then, we thought, we could return to our summer schedules:

SINGIN' IN THE RAIN

I'm singin' in the rain again.
The summer's here, the days are placid.
I'm happy as a guy can get—
Or would be if the rain weren't acid.

While we were frolicking in showers of sulfur dioxide, Judge Souter was in New Hampshire cramming for his confirmation hearing. As it turned out, he needn't have bothered. Although the senators listened politely to Souter's views on the Constitution, the only serious question—not asked explicitly, of course—was whether or not he was Robert Bork. What Souter was really saying when he seemed to be talking about philosophical values was "Look, no wispy little beard! No arrogant manner!" Senators who had pressed Bork on how he might decide specific issues didn't seem terribly curious about what Souter might do. The main element of continuity from the previous hearing was provided by Strom Thurmond of South Carolina. Whenever Thurmond's turn came, he read right through whatever questions his staff had prepared, as he had done in the Bork hearing. When a long pause indicated that the answer was over, Senator Thurmond would laboriously read the next question, and then sink back in his chair to resume the imitation he has perfected over the years of a man rather enjoying an extended coma.

During the Souter hearing it occurred to me that Senator Thurmond's reading style reminded me of someone else, and I finally realized that he read his questions precisely the same way that Margaret Tutwiler, the spokesperson for the State Department, read the official responses of the State Department to developments in the Persian Gulf. Both of them sounded like a monolingual Anglophone reading phonetically from the Hungarian.

I found myself wondering what would happen if some prankster managed to switch scripts on Strom Thurmond and Margaret Tutwiler. Asked about the fact that our spy satellites managed to report the presence of the Iraqi invasion force on the Kuwaiti border and our leaders did nothing about it—yet another indication that the government is growing more and more like one of those Hollywood movies that have brilliant special effects but end up being stupid anyway—the State Department spokesperson reads a long question concerning the *Griswold* case and whether the right of privacy is actually mentioned in the Constitution. Across town, in a Senate hearing room, Strom Thurmond reads a statement warning David Souter that any attack on Saudi Arabia will be considered an attack on the

United States. Judge Souter, in measured and rea-
soned tones, assures Senator Thurmond that he has
no intention of invading Saudi Arabia, although it
does sound like the sort of thing Robert Bork might
do.

6. Invasion

Invasion force on the Kuwaiti border? A possible attack on Saudi Arabia? That's right. The jackals had hardly slunk back into their dens when Iraq, in a Blitzkrieg attack, took over Kuwait. Most Americans knew about as much about Kuwait as they knew about David Souter. Iraq was, in a way, better known, since many people had for years confused it with Iran. In fact, a column I had written half a dozen years before put forward the theory that it was the frustration of being confused with each other that had finally driven Iraq and Iran into an otherwise inexplicable eight-year war ("How would you feel if you decided to change your name from Mesopotamia to Iraq for the usual reasons—it fits better in headlines, it sounds less foreign—and then a country right next door that has a perfectly good name of its own, Persia, started calling itself Iran?").

After the Shah's departure and the hostage crisis, Iran planted itself pretty firmly in the collective memory, and Iraq came to be confused more often with Syria, whose leader, Hafez al-Assad, seemed to be competing with Iraq's Saddam Hussein to see who could slaughter more of his own citizens. Until the summer of 1990, about the only way that Saddam and Assad could be told apart is that Saddam was the one our State Department was cozying up to and Assad was the one dismissed by the U.S. government as an unreconstructible thug. Most people can't be bothered to keep up with all the dictators the State Department is cozying up to, so when the news broke about Iraq's invasion of Kuwait, a lot of people probably blamed Hafez al-Assad. When the news mentioned Saddam by name, I could imagine a moderately well informed American citizen turning to the man next to him at the bar and saying, "Is Saddam the one who's getting a little bit of a gut or the one who looks like an accountant?"

George Bush knew which one was Saddam Hussein—the one who was getting a little bit of a gut—but he couldn't seem to pronounce Saddam's name correctly. In the face of absolutely incontrovertible evidence that Saddam is pronounced suh-DOM, with the accent on a second syllable that rhymes with Mom, Bush referred to the Iraqi president from the beginning as SAD-em, with the accent on a first syllable that rhymes, appropriately enough, with bad and cad.

Was that why Bush did it? Had some mass-psychology expert consulted by the White House decided that a subliminal rhyming connection of Saddam with bad cad would help the American people appreciate how truly wicked he was? It was known that Bush occasionally used what he thought of as tough-guy talk, such as saying to a bunch of stevedores after his 1984 vice-presidential debate with Geraldine Ferraro that he had felt the need to "kick ass." Was this some geopolitical version of a schoolyard put-down—the sort of thing that went along with "You're a brutal dictator, nya, nya, nya-nya-nya"? Not long after the invasion of Kuwait I did read somewhere that the Bush pronunciation of Saddam was actually a different word in Arabic than the correct pronunciation, and that what it meant was insulting. An expert in the low-life argot of urban Arabic was quoted as saying that in at least one city—Cairo, as I remember—SAD-em was slang for something like "insignificant shoeshine boy who leaves them streaky."

I preferred to think that George Bush might have some sort of intermittent speech impediment—maybe something that crops up now and then among people from Connecticut who spend years trying to sound as if they're from Texas. I waited hopefully for the President to appear on *NBC Nightly News* and respond to the customary respectful welcome from the anchorman by saying, "Thanks. I'm very happy to be here, Tam."

Eight or nine months later—at a time when Saddam seemed defiant despite the killing of tens of thousands of his citizens and the annihilation of his Army, I flipped on the television and caught a presidential appearance in which, in the course of calling Saddam a brutal dictator and a warmonger and a stinkpot, Bush pronounced his name correctly for the first time. "It's all over," I said aloud. I figured that Saddam must have had as the final and nonnegotiable condition for his surrender the correct pronunciation of his name by George Bush. The next day the war ended.

But before that could happen, a lot of words were written and a lot of people were killed. As the United States was preparing its response to Saddam's invasion, and most Americans were learning how to pronounce his name, the experts stepped in to explain what this was all about—which was, of course, nothing like what the moderately well informed citizen at the bar had assumed it was all about ("So this one with the gut turns out to be as much of a thug as the other one, right?"). When trouble breaks out in a part of the world about which we had enjoyed blissful ignorance, experts are always brought forward to explain to us how this has to be seen in some hitherto-unknown cultural or historical or religious context: There was this battle in 1394. There are these seven tribes. There is this ancient enmity between the lowlanders and the highlanders.

Before the Shah ran into his difficulties, for instance, Americans almost never read anything that hinted that people in Iran took their religion pretty seriously. Suddenly we had explanations of the role of the mullahs and the influence of the ayatollahs and the bitter divisions between the various branches of Islam—the latter information causing a collective sigh among those Americans who had the feeling that, after years of vague confusion, they had just begun getting the varieties of Baptists straight. When Saddam declared Kuwait part of Iraq and announced that some unlucky Americans who had been in his country at the time of the invasion would be used as human shields against retaliation, the press rounded up experts to explain why this was a lot more complicated than it looked:

HISTORICAL PERSPECTIVE

Though Westerners hold borders sacred, now
  we're told
The Arab world has never shared that point of
  view.
And hostage-taking was in Arab wars of old
Considered quite all right, so all sides took a
  few.
And autocrats they love as Englishmen love
  tea.
A holy war for Arabs never is a waste.
Iraq acts true to Lawrence (not D. H., T. E.).
I'm so relieved to know it's culturally based.

Finally, Saddam released all the hostages, perhaps not realizing that, according to some experts in the West, he was culturally entitled to hold them. It was never known precisely why he had this change of heart. Maybe Saddam, who had up until that moment seemed pretty much embarrassment-proof, was embarrassed when, on a visit to a building where some of the hostages were being held, he patted a little English boy on the head in what was supposed to be a fatherly manner and the little English boy looked at him as if he were Freddy Krueger. My theory was that the release of the hostages came because of the stream of celebrities who trooped over to Baghdad to put in a personal plea with Saddam:

WHY THE HOSTAGES WERE FREED

With hostages there,
Iraq became where
Celebrities went
On missions that meant
Some names not so new
Came back into view
As swells used their clout
To get some folks out.

The blink of an eye
Saw Jesse drop by.
Kurt Waldheim said ciao—

Respectable now.
(Good hosts don't explore
How Kurt spent his war.)
Muhammad Ali
Got some folks set free
And said he would send
His very good friend—
Knievel, no less—
For further egress.
John Connally, too,
Went home with a few.
"But what have we wrought?"
Iraq's leader thought.
"It's not really clear
What's going on here—
Real foreign affairs
Or Hollywood Squares?
Let's let these guys go.
If not, don't you know
Who'll be at our door?
Miss Zsa Zsa Gabor."

Was the United States willing to go to war to reverse the annexation of Kuwait by the One Who's Getting a Bit of a Gut? If so, why? The debate was enlivened by the fact that the White House came out with a different reason almost daily. Sometimes it was because of the oil in Kuwait. Sometimes it wasn't because of the oil in Kuwait. Sometimes it was because Saddam Hussein was such a monster that the world had to be rid of him. At one point

James Baker, the Secretary of State, said that the
reason for going to war was simply American jobs.
A citizen had trouble keeping track:

WORTH FIGHTING FOR

A citizen has trouble keeping track
Of why we may obliterate Iraq.
First Baker brands as vicious and obscene
The thought we'd fight to keep cheap gasoline.
Then Bush says oil's the issue. (We don't mind
A war for oil until it gets refined?)
He says he'll take the steps that he must take:
Our very way of life is what's at stake.
(Our "way of life"! Whatever could that mean?
Unless, of course, it means cheap gasoline.)
But then Bush says we have to draw the line
We should have drawn in 1939.
Aggression—naked—we have always loathed.
(We overlook aggression fully clothed.)
We must remove, and preferably feet first,
A monster worse than Hitler at his worst.
Then Baker, like a man who clean forgot
About this Hitler that we had to swat,
Explains we must prevail at any cost
Because if not, some jobs here could be lost.
If fighting for our jobs is now the plan,
You'd think our troops would go invade Japan.
A citizen has trouble keeping track
Of why we may obliterate Iraq.

The poem raised a question: Was I, despite the grim prospect of a major war, finding some comfort in the fact that one of the contending nations, Iraq, rhymed with practically everything? Try thinking of rhymes for Mesopotamia.

7. *Capital, Capital*

Elections don't get canceled for wars. In the fall of 1990, as Washington prepared for congressional elections, there was just the beginning whiff of anti-incumbentism in the air—a little talk about the campaign advantage incumbents have, a reminder now and then that even in the heyday of Communism the Soviet Parliament's return rate was not quite as high as the return rate of the United States Congress. The talk turned out to have little effect on the congressional elections:

AN INCUMBENT'S INTERPRETATION
OF THE 1990 CONGRESSIONAL
ELECTIONS

You'd felt a chill,
Perhaps because you'd never introduced a bill.

*(It's true that you can't find your way around
  the Hill.)
But somehow your constituents support you
  still.*

*Such bracing news!
It means that if you're noted for repulsive
  views
Or standing on the floor of Congress soaked
  with booze,
Unless you get yourself arrested you can't lose.*

*You should get by.
Yes, even if they say that you personify
The sort of hack who'll let your richest backer
  buy
Not just your vote—your coat, your shirt, your
  tie.*

*Oh, they'll attack.
But your campaign has pockets that they tend
  to lack:
A challenger can rarely match you PAC for
  PAC.
And that's the reason you'll be going back and
  back.*

*And back.
And back.
And back.*

What people in Washington do on the day after an election, of course, is to begin plotting for the next election—in this case, the presidential election of 1992. Looking around for a new party chairman, the Republicans seemed to have settled on William Bennett, who had noisily fought and ever so quietly withdrawn from the war on drugs. The theory was that the election would be fought much as the election of 1988 had been fought, with the Republican social-issues squad trying to stick the Democrats with something like being in favor of racial quotas. Bennett, a stump speaker who seemed to revel in putting forward some coded version of the proposition that the colored folks are getting all the breaks, looked like the man for that:

QUOTAS

Bill Bennett is a fellow who employs
His mouth a lot: he mostly just makes noise.
Republicans were keen to use that skill
To guarantee the next election will
Be won or lost on "Quotas: Wrong or
    Right?"—
Reminding all the voters who are white
(In case, by chance, a few of them forgot)
That they don't like the voters who are not.

But Bennett finally said the party's chair
Was not for him. Although he wouldn't care

About the need to speak of race in code,
His money needs mean he must hit the road
And make a bundle speaking for a fee.
(And yet he talks incessantly for free.)
The GOP committee isn't thrilled.
Its quota of one demagogue's unfilled.

Among rumors that Bennett was not the only person who didn't want the job, the Republicans resumed their search. They eventually came up with Clayton Yeutter, who had a name that was much more difficult to pronounce than Saddam Hussein:

ONE REPUBLICAN NATIONAL
COMMITTEE CHAIRMAN
IN SEARCH OF A PRONUNCIATION

And who might take a job most pols would want
as much as, say, a goiter?
Clayton Yeutter.
Who could they get to do the sort of task best
left to Roto-Rooter?
Clayton Yeutter.
Who'll be, to all inside the GOP, a meeter and a
greeter?
Clayton Yeutter.
Who'll pacify the right-wing nuts who call the
President a traitor?
Clayton Yeutter.
Who vows to separate the warring gangs and
calm each kick-and-biter?

> *You couldn't have said it righter. I give you*
> *Chairman Yeutter.*

The warring gangs argued mainly about social issues—particularly abortion. On issues like taxation, the Republicans seemed unified. When a few of the Democrats in Congress began talking about the possibility of putting an income tax surcharge on people who make more than a million dollars a year, both the White House and congressional Republicans responded more or less the way that little English boy had responded to the approach of Saddam Hussein. Like the Democrats, the Republicans always have a tax policy that they say will help the economy, but the Republican tax plan always seems to have the added advantage of helping rich people. The Republican view of taxes could be expressed in a simple formula: The less rich people have to pay in taxes, the better off the rest of us are.

Rich people regard this as a happy accident, a coincidence that happens to help out a group of people who couldn't be nicer. A lot of voters who aren't rich more or less agree. They have forgotten, I think, what rich people tend to do with their money:

ECONOMICS, WITH POWER STEERING

The Bush economists say folks with gobs
Should not be taxed (the gospel of the eighties)

So they'll invest the money and make jobs.
But that neglects the role of the Mercedes.

That's why this reinvestment talk is cant:
The man who makes a bunch of money lends
No start-up fund to some new widget plant.
Instead, he buys a white Mercedes-Benz.

And if you let him keep more of his pay
He won't finance a new assembly line.
He'll simply buy another one in gray.
The rich stay rich. The Germans like it fine.

The tax proposals of the Bush Administration tended to sound a lot like the tax proposals of the Reagan Administration—those glory years when most of us first heard the phrase "supply-side economics." Although I take it as a solemn duty to understand these terms so that I can explain them to my fellow citizens, Bush had succeeded Reagan before I understood what "supply-side economics" means: we have a limited supply of rich people, so we must always be on their side. Whenever Bush talked about how much better off working people would be if we just cut taxes on rich people, I kept remembering David Stockman's confession, in the early eighties, that the Reagan economic plan was, whatever the populist rhetoric that surrounded it, a way to ease the burden of taxation on the people with the largest incomes:

REMEMBER STOCKMAN

Remember Stockman, White House snitch,
Who said that tax breaks for the rich
Remained the goal of Reagan's guys,
Despite the populist disguise
Of theories (then of great renown)
About how wealth would trickle down?
And everyone attacked this man:
"One doesn't give away the plan.
The hand that feeds one one can't bite."
Well, yes, but he was also right:
We know they worked without surcease
To make the fat cats more obese.
So when George Bush says jobs will flow
And money trickle down below
If Wall Street types who buy and sell
Can keep the gains when they do well,
Remember Stockman, White House snitch.
Remember tax breaks for the rich.

One element of George Bush's tax policy turned out, upon inspection, to be the most consistent position of his long career in politics. Whenever a late-night discussion turned to questions about what made the President tick and someone asked, "What's at the core of this man?" I always had an answer: "At the core of this man is a belief in lowering the tax on capital gains."

Although Bush had changed his views on such issues as abortion and civil rights, he had held to an almost religious belief in the efficacy of lowering the tax on capital gains. Most people took it for granted that Bush's consistency on that particular issue was simply the result of living his entire life among rich people who grumbled all the time about how much of their boodle they had to turn over to a profligate government. But I always thought that Bush's belief must have been deeper than that. It seemed to me that the level of devotion he showed could best be explained by the assumption that he believed reduction of the capital-gains tax to be a sort of magic bullet that could somehow make the society he revered absolutely perfect:

EUREKA!

The drug trade will stop.
The hungry will feast.
And peace will break out
Throughout the Mideast.
The homeless will get
The homes of their dreams,
While Japanese ride
In Cutlass Supremes.
Our school kids will have
Einsteinian skills,
Plus bodies to match
The Buffalo Bills'.
Our cities rebuilt,
Our streets all secured,
Goodwill will return.

> *Oh, AIDS will be cured.*
> *It all can be done,*
> *The White House maintains:*
> *We just cut the tax*
> *On capital gains.*

In other words, Bush's beliefs might have been one version of a phenomenon of American politics that I have always thought of as monocausalism— the belief that most of what's wrong can be traced to a single factor. There are many versions of mono-causalism—there are people in Northern California who believe everything would be all right if people from Southern California simply quit stealing their water; there are people in a number of places who believe that everything would be all right if all black people were sent back to Africa—but the best known monocausalists in recent American history are the people who believed that everything would be all right if the Soviet Communist empire disappeared. According to their version of monocausalism, everything must be all right now.

8. World Leaders

So there was George Bush at the pinnacle of his powers as the ruler of the New World Order—a sort of preppie Caesar Augustus. According to the stories in the press, we were watching a triumph in personal diplomacy: a man who had over the years come to know most world leaders on a first-name basis was putting his contacts to use by organizing the armies of the world to impose a Pax Americana on the Middle East. We could imagine him on the telephone saying, with that almost endearing enthusiasm that enveloped him when he was doing something he liked, "Hiya, Maggie" and "Yo, François" and "Hey, Toshiki, how's it goin', guy?" Partway through the mobilization, the calls to Downing Street had to change to "Hey, John." Margaret Thatcher had finally been dumped, an event that I marked with a poem:

UPON MRS. THATCHER'S WITHDRAWAL

So why'd you have to be so mean, Maggie—
Like something seen on Halloween?
You always showed your pique
When speaking of the weak.
Why was the heart of you your spleen?

You would have gotten what you got, Maggie.
You could have privatized the lot.
But no one was exempt
From feeling your contempt.
Your warmth had not a single watt.

So now you've had your Waterloo, Maggie.
As colleagues try to say adieu,
They cheer you with "Hear! Hear!"s,
They wish you many years—
All spent with people mean as you.

Even aside from the Gulf War, we were living in a period of momentous change in world affairs. A leader of the Soviet Union—the head of the Communist Party—had become what amounted to an American client. In the uncertainty of what would happen in the Soviet Union—whether the old guard would really allow reform, whether any Soviet leader could permit the Soviet empire to split apart, whether *perestroika* would turn out to be a pipe dream—the United States had decided that Mikhail Gorbachev was our boy:

GORBY'S OUR BOY

This Gorbachev's our boychik even now—
Although his perestroika *team is out,*
And in the Baltics troops and tanks roll in,
And commissars again exert their clout.
But as the KGB regains its strength
And stone-faced men in overcoats get busy,
Some people here are saying of our boy,
"Yes, ours, but just who else's boychik is he?"

At the same time, there were, against all expectations, great changes going on in South Africa. For most Americans, the Soviet Union and South Africa had been considered unmitigated bad guys for so long that they seemed immutable. Yet here were both of them changing at the same time, and both through what seemed to be the effort of one strong-willed, confident leader. How could this happen? In each case, of course, you could list fifteen or twenty MLs of historical and political and economic factors. (An ML is a unit of measurement equal to the combined theorizing of one panel discussion of specialists on the *MacNeil/Lehrer Newshour.*) But could there also be something personal that tied these two ostensibly disparate situations together? I was thinking about that one morning while I was shaving, and, suddenly catching my reflection in

the mirror, I thought I knew. I wrote a poem, which
probably should have been called "Poetic Inspiration while Shaving" but was called instead "The
Secret of Leadership":

THE SECRET OF LEADERSHIP

Two countries were, at best, adrift.
Two leaders made the basic shift
They had to make to make things work.
There's Gorbachev, and there's De Klerk.
But why these two? What made them brave
Enough to say the way to save
Their countries was to change the game?
It's in their hair, or lack of same.
The theory's this: If you have hair,
Your blood takes vital fluids there,
Which otherwise you'd use to fuel
The will that made you born to rule.
It does sound strange. I think it's true.
If you were bald, then so would you.

The publication of that poem brought some in-
quiries from my friends and acquaintances. Was
there any evidence of a connection between leadership and people who were overweight or people
who had more or less given up flossing or people
who could never hit the curve? The best I could
come up with was some evidence, gathered from
my reading of various glossy periodicals, that
plumpness was edging back into style:

ON THE RETURN OF THE
FULLER FIGURE

A woman's shape again is cause for joy:
She's not a boy!
The hourglass is back, and fashion groans
At skin and bones.
So if your wife has grown a little plumper,
You shouldn't dump her.
And if your gut rests softly on your desk,
You're Rubenesque.

Eventually, of course, it became obvious that the Evil Empire was not just fraying around the edges but in complete collapse. Sooner or later, Gorbachev stepped down—Boris Yeltsin replaced him as our boychik—and the Russian government actually outlawed the Communist Party. For those of us who had lived our entire adult lives under the assumption that the center ring of international affairs would always be occupied by the battle between the Communism of the Soviet Union and American free enterprise, this was mind-boggling:

BASIC ASSUMPTION SHAKEN

So Russia is trashing the Party.
I'm sorting out just what this means.
Could the Pope be a little bit Baptist?
Do bears in the woods have latrines?

I couldn't help thinking about the people in the West who had staked their lives on the proposition that Soviet Communism was the certain way of the future. I couldn't help thinking of one of those English spies who had betrayed his country and then skipped to Moscow—accepting the commission as a major in the KGB that had been held for him all those years, settling into some drab Moscow flat where there was always static when you tried to get the cricket scores on the BBC World Service. What would he have said when it all came tumbling down? "Well, it seemed like a good idea at the time."

SPIES RECONSIDERED

The Moscow news has made it quite a strain
To contemplate Guy Burgess and Maclean.
For now their party's over, always will be.
And think of all that spying! Think of Philby!
We have to ask ourselves: 'Twas all for naught
They did those things they really hadn't ought?

For just about everybody else, though, the end of the Cold War seemed like glorious news. In Eastern Europe, people were dancing in the streets. In the United States, although the Gulf War had cut off some of the more optimistic talk about a peace dividend, there was at least some hope that an occasional sword might be beaten into a plowshare. Somehow, though, the most expensive project of all—the Strategic Defense Initiative, or Star Wars—seemed unchanged. Even after George Bush signed an historic pact on nuclear weapons with the former Soviet Union, SDI lingered, like a dinner guest who hangs around after the party is over—and keeps eating.

ON THE PRESIDENT'S NUCLEAR INITIATIVE

A start! And maybe, by and by,
A pact that all can ratify
Will make an end. We'll say goodbye
To bombs of mass destruction. Try
Imagining how blue the sky
When there's a way to verify—
Some technilectracratic spy—
That they're all gone. Not one can fly.
We'll hear a universal sigh.
A tear will drop from every eye.
With no more missile heads to buy,
We'll concentrate on SDI.

9. A Deadline Poet's War

FRAGMENT OF TRANSCRIPT
FROM NEGOTIATIONS WITH
SADDAM HUSSEIN ON
WITHDRAWAL FROM KUWAIT

"You'll have to go."

"The river with your stinking blood will flow as Islam brings you monumental woe, annihilating Allah's every foe with every fiendish torture apropos: we'll lop your heads off with a mighty blow, then chop you finer than a sloppy joe!"

"Is that a no?"

THURSDAY NIGHT WAR

Miraculously, we at home could see
That first attack on Israel on TV—
Brave correspondents standing at the scene,
Interpreting what sounds we heard might
*   mean,*
Providing battle details all night long.
Of course, a lot of what they said was wrong:
That Tel Aviv was hit by poison gas,
That Israel's planes had gone to kick some
*   ass.*
It's known that war is chaos, not just hell.
Impressions that are instant rarely tell
Us much about what happened that is true.
That usually takes a longer point of view.
But now each network has and so employs
The satellite and other costly toys.
I don't suggest that we get rid of these.
Just keep in mind: they ain't Thucydides.

RESPITE

Domestically, poor Bush was in the loo.
The budget mess, recession, and a stew
Of problems—drugs and health care, to name
*   two—*
Gave evidence that Bush's White House crew
Had not a clue of what to do.

Now news shows show no homeless on a grate.
They show our triumphs as we devastate
Iraq with weapons all appreciate.
Because Bush went to war to free Kuwait,
He has a great approval rate.

But when we show Saddam Hussein the door,
We'll still have problems here we can't ignore.
In fact, by then we could have many more.
The White House, just as baffled as before,
Might have to score another war.

A SHORT MILITARY BIOGRAPHY OF SADDAM HUSSEIN

This guy who often said he'd smash us flat in
*   one battle*
Turned out to be what Texans call all hat and
*   no cattle.*

SUGGESTED CHEERS FOR THE BROADWAY TICKER-TAPE VICTORY PARADE

Who's
The only four-star general we've got
Who tries to be a modern Lancelot,

Although he looks a lot like Willard Scott?
Yeaaaaa, Norm! Big as a dorm! Rah, rah!

Who's
The guy who made us gladder by the hour
That those in charge of judging John G. Tower
Had sent the little fellow to the shower?
Yeaaaaa, Cheney! Rarely zany! Rah, rah!

Who's
The first pol at the Saudi aerodrome,
The first to wish Israeli friends shalom—
Distracting from the crooked stuff at home?
Yeaaaaa, D'Amato! Sleazeball obbligato! Rah,
*   rah!*

VICTORY PARADES:
A COWBOY'S LAMENT

So why no parade for Grenada?
No cheers for the lads and the lasses
Who took freedom's flag to Grenada
And whipped them Grenadians' asses.

We don't take no sass from Iraqis.
We fought them. We gave them no quarter.
We made real short work of them Arabs.
The work in Grenada was shorter.

I love all our troops from the desert.
I'd give them all overnight passes.
But what of the troops in Grenada
Who whipped them Grenadians' asses?

THE KURDS ARE INTERNAL

The Kurds are internal, tra-la, tra-la,
The Kurds are internal affairs.
Their slaughter's a pity, tra-la, tra-la.
But hardly our problem. It's theirs.
We'll feed them and clothe them, tra-la, tra-la,
Then back to their homeland they'll wend.
Till next time we tell them, tra-la, tra-la,
To rise and be slaughtered again.
With troubles eternal, tormentors infernal,
It's still just fraternal, tra-la, tra-la.
The Kurds are internal affairs.

COLIN POWELL RECONSIDERED

A new book says that Colin Powell
Last August was a dove-like fowl:
He said he didn't see the rush
To bomb them into cornmeal mush.
Although he seems too tough to dis, he
May now be branded as a sissy.

10. And Why Not Poet Laureate?

ON NOT MAKING THE CUT

They've named another poet laureate.
It's not me yet.

I do want to applaud him from the bench—
To be a mensch.

And yet I've been ignored so many times.
And my stuff rhymes!

Hey! Maybe that's my problem—rhyme's a
  curse.
I'll try blank verse:

Listen, selectors, I'd make a great
poet laureate, and I'm not the kind
of guy who would get uppity if you asked

him to knock out eight or ten lines for
the First Lady's birthday or anything like
that. Think about it. Thanks.

This was not the first time that the subject of the
poet-laureate job had come up around our house.
In 1988, when Robert Penn Warren was selected
as the first poet laureate—until then, a similar position had been called something like the Poetry
Consultant to the Library of Congress—I decided
to write a column celebrating his appointment and
to include a short congratulatory poem, in the form
of a cheer:

Who has poetic gifts scarcer than the tooth of a
  hen?
Robert Penn!

I might as well admit that, since Warren's appointment was only for a year or two, I also used the
occasion to mention my availability for the post the
next time it came open. Why not? One reason my
wife was able to think of was that I had never published a poem. I don't think she meant this as a
quibble. Just in case, I thought the column might
be a good opportunity to work in a poem or two,
to give the people in Washington some idea of the
sort of work I was up to. I included, for instance,
some lyrics from *If There's No Nova Scotia in Nova
Scotia, There Can't Be Any French Fries in France*,
the film that is generally considered the highlight

of my song-writing career. The lyrics happened to be from a song about a fish smoker who dreams of becoming a country singing star, and I admitted that in the back of my mind I might have considered the possibility that the subject could be of interest to a senator from a fish-smoking state who happened to be on the committee with oversight of the Library of Congress:

Smoking fish just ain't my dish. I want to be a
*   star.*
I want to sing some lonesome country ballads,
Not smoke this fish for people's salads.
I've got some country stories I could tell.
In a roadside dump this country cracker'll
Be better off than smoking mackerel.
I've got to leave this awful fishy smell.
Smoking fish just ain't my dish. I want to be a
*   star.*

I also included in the column a poem about mime —a poem I thought would strike a sympathetic note with just about anybody:

Nobody really likes mime.
Nobody knows what they're showing.
Boat rowing? Lawn mowing? Grass growing?
If he's paying somebody a peso
To make him some chile con queso,
Couldn't he simply just say so?
A few words would help—can't they see?

What could the cost to them be?
Speech in this country is free!
Nobody knows what they're playing.
Spring haying? Croqueting? Egg laying?
There's really no reason or rhyme.
Nobody really likes mime.

In the spring of 1991, after I had been a deadline poet for seven or eight months, it was time for another poet laureate to be chosen. At this point there could be no quibble about my not having published any poetry. Still, my telephone did not ring. I suppose I must have seemed dispirited, because my wife said, "Look at it this way: you're not exactly a poet. What you write is light verse."

I thought about that awhile. I wasn't sure I found it terribly comforting. "I suppose my day will come when they decide to have a light-versist laureate," I finally said. "Is that what you mean?"

"Well, also—"

"I hope we can complete this conversation without the use of the word 'doggerel,' " I said. I think of "deadline poet" as the appropriate job description for what I do, although I haven't reached the point of describing myself that way on visa applications or landing cards.

A deadline-poet laureate? Well, I wouldn't have pushed for it, but why not? By chance, Queen Elizabeth II, a representative of the monarchy that had employed the original poet laureate, happened to be in the country, moving stiffly from stiff ceremony to stiff ceremony. Just to demonstrate the sort of effort that could be expected of a deadline-poet laureate, I wrote a poem about her visit to a public housing project in Washington—a visit during which she got a bear hug from a community leader who was apparently unaware that one does not touch the monarch:

ON THE QUEEN'S VISIT
TO ALICE FRAZIER'S HOUSE
IN SOUTHEAST WASHINGTON

When Mrs. F. embraced the Queen,
Folks jumped, as if there'd been a mugging.
The rules say royals can't be touched.
But Lord, that Queen could use some hugging!

The more I thought about it, the more certain I was that a deadline poet is actually the logical sort of versifier to be poet laureate—much more logical than the sort of poet my wife has the unfortunate habit of calling a grown-up poet. As I pointed out in the poem that could be considered my application, a deadline poet would not consider, say, a birthday poem beneath him. I made the transition, after all, from special-occasion poetry to deadline poetry; I could just as easily go back again. Even as a deadline poet, I was accustomed to doing celebratory poems—in the spirit that a poet laureate in Great Britain might do a poem on, say, the Queen's Silver Jubilee. Around the time of Queen

Elizabeth's visit, I had done just that sort of poem on the progress being made by people like Jim and Sarah Brady in getting a gun-control bill through Congress:

WE'VE GOT THE GUN NUTS ON THE RUN

We've got the gun nuts on the run.
Their power has begun to fade
Before the Bradys' brave crusade.
They feel abandoned and betrayed
By pols whose bills they've always paid.
The strain among them has displayed
Some rifts along their barricade.
We've got the gun nuts on the run.

I hope they don't turn and shoot us.

In the poet-laureate tradition, I often did poems on national holidays. That year, for instance, I had done a poem about Father's Day—the day when American fathers traditionally emerge temporarily from their assigned role as the bumbling guy in the cardigan who exists to be manipulated by his wife and children:

FATHER'S DAY IS GONE

Father's Day is gone. It's over.
Dad was briefly in the clover—

Feeling wise, a valued leader
Who deserved that power weeder.
Cracking wry, a bit like Cos, he
Now reverts—it's back to Ozzie.

I had also followed the poet-laureate custom of writing regular poems about the head of state, not all of them insulting. Shortly after the new poet laureate was named, there was a minor rumble about the theory of one historian that Zachary Taylor—the twelfth President of the United States, a former general who had been pretty much forgotten by everyone but schoolchildren forced to memorize the names of the Presidents—had died not from heat stroke or overeating, as had long been assumed, but from poison. The historian managed to get Taylor's body exhumed, a hundred and forty-one years after his death. Significantly, the poet laureate of the United States did not care to comment on this historical event. I did:

ZACHARY TAYLOR
R.(Mostly)I.P.

1850
Taylor, called Old Rough and Ready,
Had a gut-ache. Once in bed, he
Howled with pain, and cursed, and thrashed
   about.
More than Taylor's gorge was rising.

Then he started in demising.
Gluttony was blamed: he'd just pigged out.

1991
"Poison!" folks said. On this basis,
He was dug up, checked for traces.
(Zach by then was hardly at his peak.)
Finding none in or around him,
They replaced him where they'd found him.
Zachary was famous for a week.

11. *Some Candidates, Finally*

By that summer, the summer of 1991, my brethren in the Washington press corps were concerned about how few candidates had been spotted in Iowa setting up organizations and getting a little name recognition for the February caucuses. The delay in campaign activity had robbed our crowd of the opportunity to register its quadrennial complaints about how the modern presidential race begins too early and lasts too long. Ordinarily, this was the time in the electoral cycle when political columns were filled with almost audible sighs, as columnists toted up all of the bombast we had already heard from presidential candidates and how much there was left to hear in the fourteen or fifteen months before the election brought blessed relief. How could a columnist claim to be sick of the whole business already if the business hadn't even begun?

The ladies and gentlemen of the press were not

the only people lamenting the absence of political oratory in Iowa church basements and service-club lunches. In the Corn State, the first skirmishes for the party nominations have evolved into a small industry—a smaller industry than corn but one, it was thought, that was not subject to the vagaries of bug infestations or commodity-market slides or the weather. The men in their feed-company hats who gather at the cafés of little Iowa towns for coffee and lamentations normally spend a lot of their time anticipating disaster from one source or another, and, as the first hint of fall was felt in the air, I could imagine them simply folding into their gloomy dialogue the prospect of a particularly thin crop of primary candidates:

"This kind of weather means no rain when we need it, sure as shootin'."

"Think we'll get any Republicans?"

"Bush is at seventy-eight."

"A bushel of what's at seventy-eight?"

"No, George Bush is at 78 percent approval rating. That means no Republicans. Maybe no Democrats."

"It'll be as dry as a Baptist wedding. Mark my word."

"I'm for Bush. In '88 he complimented the wife on her tuna casserole."

"Eighty-eight? A bushel of what's at eighty-eight?"

If you look back at that period, it isn't hard to see that we hadn't completely emerged from the

Summer of the False Positive. Because Americans rally around any President in time of international crisis and because the Gulf War seemed to be a great triumph, George Bush looked unbeatable. Most economists were predicting that the economy would recover in time to prevent the Democrats from making an election issue out of it. There was an assumption that the Republicans would be able to lean on one of their "wedge issues"—quotas, maybe, or "family values"—to maintain their hold on the Reagan Democrats. Given all that, the stories about potential Democratic candidates were mostly about who had decided not to run. Richard Gephardt decided not to run. Bill Bradley decided not to run. In Iowa, hotel proprietors and rental-car agencies and printers and radio-advertising salesmen were in the position of farmers in an icy spring, waiting impatiently to get the crops in the ground.

Every time someone from what the press called the "first tier" of candidates dropped out, the speculation would settle on another likely Democrat, who, after a week or so of consideration, would decide not to run. One of the most prominent of the wonder-of-the-week candidates was Senator Jay Rockefeller, of West Virginia. He decided not to run:

ADIEU, MR. R.

He conjures up the hollers
And hills of West Virginny:

Although he's not so poor,
At least he's tall and skinny.

For what they call a balanced race,
He was a fine augmenter:
With Jesse Left, and Bentsen Right,
And Rockefeller Center.

Then Bentsen decided not to run. Then even Jesse Jackson, who always runs, decided not to run. Political reporters—who even in a foreshortened campaign season would have to sit through eight or ten months of campaign oratory—were dismayed that Jackson, by far the most entertaining speaker, was out of contention:

ON CAMPAIGN RHETORIC

Yes, those who savor campaign talking
Lament the fact that Jesse's walking.
A race, they think, can't be historic
Without some waxing metaphoric.
They fear that now some mumbling twerp'll
Campaign with phrases lacking purple.

But

There're other Democrats, I'm finding,
With skills that get that stem a-winding.
This Cuomo's stock goes up the more he
Displays his gift for oratory.

Of Clinton, we know (to our sorrow)
That he can talk into tomorrow.
And Harkin, Iowa folks will mention,
When wound up gets the hogs' attention.

But

Bush may have a speaking style as smooth as
*   Scotch-and-soda:*
"Quotaquotaquotaquotaquotaquotaquota."

Finally, sometime after Labor Day, there were
half a dozen Democratic candidates. It was, as they
say in politics, a horse race:

THE IOWA DERBY

There's Clinton and Wilder and Kerrey and
*   Brown*
And Harkin and Tsongas, of course.
So why did we grumble for so many months
This horse race was lacking a horse?
We might scratch a couple, for one is a flake
And rumor says one is a letch.
But even with fewer we've still got enough
To splatter some mud in the stretch.

The candidate I predicted might be scratched
because of rumors of lechery was, of course, the
candidate who was to become President of the
United States. I could claim that this was merely

an example of what we deadline poets call rhyming license—"letch" did seem to be the obvious word to rhyme with "stretch"; no one has ever dropped from contention in a presidential primary because he turned out to be a "kvetch" or because he made the voters "retch"—but I might as well admit that it was a simple mistake. When those rumors about Clinton's wandering eye and his avoidance of the draft became public a few months later, during the New Hampshire primary, I agreed with all the Washington pundits who were predicting that he couldn't recover. There was the Double Whammy Rule to consider—the rule holding that a presidential candidate (seen here as a wildebeest being pursued by a pack of wild dogs) might be able to absorb one serious wound but would be brought down by a second. There was also the Monologue Rule, according to which no one can survive as a serious candidate once he becomes a catch line in the monologues of the sort of lounge comics who ordinarily lean heavily on bad language and jokes about drugs. The Double Whammy Rule and the Monologue Rule had proven fallible. The rule that Washington pundits are never wrong is, of course, still intact.

The eventual assembling of a field of Democratic candidates did not necessarily reverse the pessimism of the guys in the feed-company hats. In the first place, the equivalent of a lot of growing days had been lost. In the second place, the fact that Tom Harkin, one of Iowa's own senators, had declared himself a candidate meant that it might be less important for a candidate to concentrate on caucuses that were certain to be dominated by Harkin anyway:

> *He'd surely be the Corn State's favorite son,*
> *Which could give others one excuse to shun*
> *The caucus circuit in that worthy state—*
> *And all that meat loaf, which, in truth, they*
>   *hate.*

Also, there was some question about whether the field would be complete at the caucuses. There was still a lot of talk about the combative and complicated governor of New York, Mario Cuomo—a man who had been portrayed as essentially Hamlet with a chip on his shoulder. Cuomo was sometimes talking about making the race, and sometimes talking about not making the race, and mostly talking about how reporters had misinterpreted his previous, perfectly clear statement of intent:

AFTER SEEING MARIO CUOMO INTERVIEWED ON TELEVISION

> *He seems so assured. What a brain!*
> *Then why does he harbor such doubt—*
> *Reminding us all of that Dane?*
> *Well, here's what the doubt is about:*
> *Can he make it through a campaign*
> *Without punching somebody out?*

12. Enter Clarence Thomas

THE SUPREMES

Well, first they found a woman who's really not
  so sure
Abortion's for a woman to decide.
And then they got a black man who thinks that
  special help
For black folks should be canceled
  countrywide.
They're looking for a Jewish judge who really
  sees the point
Of keeping Jews away from one's resort.
And then a smart Latino who'd like the border
  closed.
At last we'll have a truly balanced Court.

Was that fair? Well, maybe not to Sandra Day
O'Connor—who, on the abortion question and

other issues, turned out to be in a centrist group on the Court that was called moderate by some and by others "not overtly insane." I think it was fair to Clarence Thomas. Anybody who had any doubt about why Thomas was selected by the Bush Administration should have had none at all left after George Bush—in one of those casual pieces of mendacity in which politicians say the precise opposite of what is true, as if challenging the public to think otherwise—said that Thomas's nomination had nothing to do with race but came about simply because he was the most qualified person in the country to be on the Supreme Court. What else could Bush have said without becoming a backer of affirmative action? So the entire episode started off with a simple lie, and no one should have been surprised that a lot more lies were told before it was over.

THE ART OF CONVERSATION

Oh, once we talked of many things.
We talked of movies, plays, and books.
We argued politics all night.
We graded pols as knaves or schnooks.
We talked of baseball, food, and wine,
Discussed if acupuncture hurts.
Our conversations measured all:
Say, breadth of vision, length of skirts.
We planned the future of the world.
To shut us up, you'd have to bomb us.

But now we talk of just two things:
Anita Hill and Clarence Thomas.

Once the Senate Judiciary Committee had held its hearings on the accusations against Thomas made by Anita Hill, I acknowledged in a column that I had been part of an office pool on which senator would be the most revolting. "I drew Teddy Kennedy and thought I was in clover," I reported. "I was hoping that Senator Kennedy might unburden himself of some pious words on the horrors of sexual harassment, but Kennedy kept what they call in Washington a low profile. In fact, he seemed to be trying to lower his profile so that it was just under the top of the table." There was no serious argument about awarding the pool money to the guy who had drawn Senator Alan Simpson, although the guy in my office who had drawn Orrin Hatch did keep muttering, "Smarmy demeanor ought to count for something." In an imitation of the late senator from Wisconsin that lacked only the five o'clock shadow for total verisimilitude, Simpson held in his hands what he said were letters from unnamed people saying things about Anita Hill that were too sinister to mention. Since this was the second straight time that Simpson had been declared most revolting in one of our office pools—he won during the Gulf War by accusing Peter Arnett, the CNN correspondent, of being a Vietcong sympathizer—we decided to make him ineligible for the next pool.

Although Senator Kennedy hadn't had much to

say on the subject, the hearings made sexual harassment a widely discussed topic. I tried to imagine what some of the senatorial discussions were like, away from the hearing room:

A SENATOR AND A TOP AIDE DISCUSS THE ISSUE OF SEXUAL HARASSMENT

The senator (distinguished, Romanesque)
Assures his aide (quite bright, and statuesque)
Harassment's truly dreadful, just grotesque.
He speaks while chasing her around the desk.

Clarence Thomas, of course, was confirmed and, to nobody's surprise, began demonstrating on the Court that nothing Antonin Scalia could think of was too reactionary for him to go along with. Anita Hill went back to being a law professor, and then gradually began appearing in public to speak on sexual harassment. As it turned out, any number of female candidates in the next congressional election would mention the Thomas-Hill hearings as the event that made them resolve to run—an indication, maybe, that the discussion of which member of the Senate Judiciary Committee was most revolting had been going on in places other than just our office.

13. *Thinking about November*

About a year before a presidential election, one of the familiar tendencies of people who observe government and politics—the tendency to interpret any event according to how it might affect the next election—becomes intensified. The Washington soothsayers turn an event around in their hands for hours, feeling for a bump here or a line there that may say something about who went up a tick and who went down a tick. Does a local election somewhere reflect anything about the President's standing? Does the passage of an important package of legislation—or the defeat of an important package of legislation—in some state say anything about whether the governor of that state may run for the presidency? In the fall of 1991, of course, George Bush was still riding high. The first disquieting news came from Pennsylvania, where Dick Thornburgh,

Bush's Attorney General, had been expected to waltz into the Senate in a special election:

THE RESULTS FROM PENNSYLVANIA

Well armed with Bush's fond esteem,
Dick Thornburgh left this gray regime,
Went home to take the job they'd proffered,
And ran straight into Harris Wofford.
Dick thought it was a cinch. Instead,
This Wofford handed him his head.
The lesson? Some said Dick got cocky,
Thus Wofford could be seen as Rocky
(The boxer, not the Veep and guv
Who now looks down from heav'n above).
And some say Bush has clay for feet.
Whatever's true, Dick's on the street.

One piece of legislation that was analyzed largely according to the role it might play in the 1992 presidential election was a civil-rights bill designed to facilitate lawsuits from people who believed they had been discriminated against in the workplace. President Bush had vetoed a similar measure, and threatened to veto this one, on the ground that it was a quota bill. Business leaders and the civil-rights coalition were at the point of working out a compromise on the new bill—a compromise that would have presumably eased the fears of both those who were worried about discrimination and those who were worried about quotas—when their efforts were sabotaged by John Sununu and C. Boyden Gray, the White House counsel, in what was interpreted as an effort to preserve the quota issue for the election. At least the punching-bag-shaped Sununu and the shambling Gray, known to some behind his back as Uriah Creep, provided some fodder for political cartoonists: picturing the two together called to mind a malevolent version of Laurel and Hardy. When the President finally had to sign a compromise bill, Gray, like a spin doctor who'd become high on his own medicine, circulated the draft of an executive order that would have ended government affirmative action programs—a race appeal so overt Bush had to disavow it publicly. At the signing, the White House tried pretending that Gray didn't exist, like a family that prepares for important visitors by locking loony Uncle Harry in the cellar.

GRAY AREA

The White House is in disarray.
That megaklutz, C. Boyden Gray,
Can't seem to find a way to say
"We mean to keep the blacks at bay"
Without igniting quite a fray.
With such a message to convey,
A messenger can go astray.
He has to find a subtle way
To send it out—not overplay,
And sound just like the KKK.

The subtlety of all this may
Just be too much for Boyden Gray.

In which case, they'll have to find
somebody else to do it.

As everyone looked toward the 1992 elections, the Republicans had to signal that they understood the code, but they also had to distance themselves from David Duke, who was running for governor on the Republican ticket in Louisiana. Duke, who had managed to get some cosmetic surgery done on both his face and his ideas, was sounding more and more like a Willie Horton Republican:

ON DAVID DUKE AS REPUBLONAZI

The GOP denies
The slightest Dukish ties.
They're sorry that he ran.
They loathe the Ku Klux Klan.
And yet it's true that he
And they (the GOP)
When stepping to the mike
Do tend to sound alike:
"Blame middle-class defeats
On quotas, welfare cheats."
One word they both hold back
Is what they both mean: black.
The codes give them away:
He's got their DNA.

It's funny who you meet
By peeking 'neath the sheet.

As events transpired, George Bush's campaign
would not be run from the White House by the
man often credited with saving the faltering Bush
effort in 1988—John Sununu. The previous spring
it had been revealed that Sununu was in the habit
of taking military planes to the dentist in New
Hampshire and White House limos to stamp shows
in New York. Here was a man so interested in his
own importance that he would rather spend five or
six hours in traffic in a White House limo than be
exposed to lesser mortals on the shuttle for an hour.
I had suggested that the legendary New Hampshire
license plate motto, "Live Free or Die," be changed
to "Fly Free or Die." Other than that, I commented
only with a short reprise of "If You Knew What
Sununu," the first verse of which said

If you knew what Sununu
Now knows about getting a plane,
You'd have to acquire no more frequent-flier
Awards for your summer in Spain.

But the jackals in Washington were baying at Sununu's heels. (Yes, jackals bay; it sounds very much
like the sound that word processors make.) It was
time for his friends in Washington to rally around
him, and that left him pretty much alone. White
House advisers argued that Sununu had become a

liability. Finally, George Bush, known as a man who hated to fire people, showed him the door.

Bush was not the only one who had been reluctant to have Sununu leave. What was *I* supposed to do without him? He was, after all, my poetic inspiration. I felt the way Shakespeare would have felt if he had received a letter from the Dark Lady's mother: "My daughter, the Dark Lady, will no longer be available to inspire your sonnets. P.S. You ought to be ashamed of yourself."

I hadn't been steadily writing poems about Sununu all this time, but I had been comforted by his presence. He was a central figure when I tried to envision scenes of White House decision-making. When he and Richard Darman, the budget director, were dispatched to negotiate with Congress about the budget, I tried to imagine how George Bush, a man whose vast experience in government had obviously taught him that congressmen can be easily offended if not given the respect they believe to be their due, came to the decision to send those particular ambassadors: "We got anybody real arrogant we can send over there?" Bush says. "We got anybody whose main goal in any situation is to demonstrate that he considers everyone else in the room to be small and stupid?"

"Well, Chief, there's Bob Bork, but I don't think we can get him. He's still sort of mad about last time."

"Well, let's send Sununu. We'll send Darman

along with him, just in case he forgets to be con-
descending."

Along with Darman, Sununu had also been a central figure in the palace intrigues that brightened
up the gray of the Bush Administration a bit with
tiny flecks of blood. I had always counted on him
when the backstabbing began:

DISHARMONY AMONG THE PRESIDENT'S MEN

Sununu and Darman can never see harm in
their scheming for personal gain.
Newt Gingrich of Georgia, that corn-pone
L. Borgia, enjoys causing both of them pain.
New Paradigm wackos, relentless as backhoes,
would shove Darman down a crevasse.
It's hardly smooth sailing, revealing a failing:
Bush doesn't know how to kick ass.

Far from demonstrating any concern about those
who valued him as the one dependable punching
bag in the White House, though, Sununu had
seemed intent on doing himself in. Around Thanks-
giving of 1991, he'd said that a reference in one of
President Bush's speeches to the possibility of a cap
on credit-card interest rates—a reference that Sununu had been suspected of inserting, and one that
provoked a deep dip in the stock market—had been
ad-libbed by the President. In other words, he

broke the one cardinal rule of his job: You never blame the boss. Suddenly he was out of there, replaced by Samuel Skinner, who seemed to be yet another gray Republican in his middle years.

TWO POEMS (FOR THE PRICE OF ONE) ON SUNUNU'S REPLACEMENT

INTELLECTUALLY
Republicans portray him as the party's whiz:
Not dumb enough to brag about how smart he
  is.

AESTHETICALLY
It isn't clear this Skinner is a winner.
But he's thinner.

14. A One-Termer?

In Washington, Sununu's departure was taken as an indication that the warning whistle first sounded by the Pennsylvania senatorial election was being heard in the White House. It was beginning to seem conceivable that George Bush, who once had an approval rating that might have been envied by Joe DiMaggio, could be a one-term President. With the economy getting worse rather than better, it had begun to look as if the war cry that the Reagan-Bush campaign used so effectively against Jimmy Carter in 1980—Are you better off than you were four years ago?—might be used against Bush himself. Even the prosperity of the eighties had begun to look a little different, as the debt burden of mergers caught up with some companies and statistics became available on who had actually emerged from that glitz blizzard with more wealth and who hadn't.

THE EIGHTIES RE-EXAMINED

"It all will trickle down," the boomster said.
The eighties were when no one but a kook
Would mention that the poor got poorer while
The rich lived more and more like King
  Farouk.

Statistics now show where the boom dough
  went.
The middle classes hardly gained a nickel.
Two-thirds went to the richest one percent.
A breakthrough: we produced an upward
  trickle.

The White House was still saying that times were not as hard as all that. I could imagine the President's advisers meeting secretly in the White House situation room to figure out what to do about the economy—secretly, because they didn't want the general public to know that the economy was in the tank. This had to be the hardest government secret to keep since Henry Kissinger, Sununu's predecessor as the really smart guy in the outfit, carried on the secret bombing of Cambodia, hoping that the Cambodians wouldn't notice.

As I envisioned the scene, everyone at the meeting agrees that the first step toward fixing the economy well enough to win the 1992 election, now only a year away, is to encourage Americans to go out during the Christmas shopping season and buy a lot of stuff they can't afford. According to one of the root theories of the American capitalist system (expressed here in terms that non-economists can understand), being hopelessly in debt gives people confidence.

How do you inspire shoppers to snatch the shelves clean? The White House decides that the President could accomplish this with what the economists call a photo-op pump primer. But what sort of presidential purchase would infect the general population with shopping fever? Normally White House advisers might set up a focus group of ordinary citizens to find that answer, but if they did that, the word might get out that there was something wrong with the economy. So they ask one of their own number what he would consider an inspirational Christmas gift, and the one they happen to ask is C. Boyden Gray. "What would turn you on, C. Boyden?" they ask. "What would make you think Santa has made this the bestest Christmas ever?"

"White athletic socks?" C. Boyden Gray says. "I go for white athletic socks."

Perfect! A photo opportunity with the President buying white athletic socks! Then, as the advisers envision the plan working, millions of Americans say, "Well, if the President has enough confidence in the economy to buy athletic socks, there's nothing to worry about. I'm going to shop till I drop."

Even as I imagined this scenario I realized that it was preposterous. But how else are we to explain what happened? How else are we to explain that, at the beginning of the Christmas shopping season of 1991, the President of the United States, accompanied by beaming White House aides and a gaggle of photographers, walked into the J. C. Penney store in a large shopping mall in Maryland and ceremoniously purchased four pairs of white athletic socks?

Considering how puzzled the President later seemed at the failure of the recession to end, it has even occurred to me that, standing at the J. C. Penney cash register as the sale was being rung up, Bush might have thought to himself, Well, that takes care of that. The economy was fixed, and he could turn to his real love, foreign affairs.

By the closing months of 1991, any doubts about whether the Cold War with the Soviet Union was truly over had to be put to rest, because the Soviet Union had ceased to exist. Mikhail Gorbachev, the Soviet leader George Bush had been elected to negotiate with, had, whether he had intended to or not, presided over the dissolution of the Evil Empire:

GORBACHEV'S REWARD

He started down that slope so slippery.
Though talking toughly to the Gipper, he
Uncorked the bottle with the genie
Who showed the mighty bear was teeny.

And now his union's disuniting.
Does Gorbachev need some requiting
From those he previously was fighting?
Should Queen Elizabeth do some knighting?

Or Bush could now, at Cold War's end,
Decide to send this newfound friend
A gift for tumbling Eastern blocs:
Four pairs of white athletic socks.

If the Cold War between the United States and the Soviet Union was over, and the Soviet Union no longer existed, it stood to reason that the United States had won the Cold War—sort of. President Bush announced plans to go to Japan as part of a triumphant worldwide tour—the same sort of tour, it seemed to me, that Muhammad Ali had taken many years before, after he won the heavyweight championship. "I'm the world champion," Ali had explained at the time. "So I wanted to see the world I was champion of." Before the preparations had been completed, though, it became obvious that there was a problem: the white-athletic-socks strategy for ending the recession hadn't worked. A lot of people thought that Bush should stay home and concentrate on the economy—shop for sneakers, maybe, or a windbreaker. Bush was intent on going, so the trip was, as they say in the amusement-park business, rethemed: the White House let it be known that the presidential tour would not be about cementing relations with our allies as we entered the New World Order but about "jobs, jobs, jobs."

FAR EASTERN TRAVEL

The trip that Bush first scheduled, then
*   postponed,*
Had been designed to show our George
*   enthroned*
As monarch of the newly ordered world.
But then a monkey wrench was rudely hurled
Into those plans: some frank, heroic soul
Told Bush that half the country's on the dole,
And that the President's the one who grapples
With ways to keep the swells from selling
*   apples.*

The trip went on. They simply changed the
*   theme.*
He'll bring home jobs, they said. The team
He'd take along to help with this charade:
Important CEOs, all overpaid.
The trip became a metaphor, no less,
For policies that helped produce our mess,
By following that U.S. business rule:
Why don't we just repackage, not retool?

The trip was an absolute disaster. The salaries of the CEOs became a subject for intense national scrutiny. The spotlight provided by coverage of the trip did not illuminate the unfair trade practices

American car manufacturers had been whining about as much as it did the ineptitude of their export operations. The cars they had been trying to sell in Japan, for instance, hadn't even been equipped with steering wheels on the side that the Japanese, who drive on the left-hand side of the road, might find convenient. I tried to imagine what happened around 1986 when Ralph, the Marketing Vice President of a Detroit auto manufacturer, went to the Chief Executive Officer (Mo) and the Chief Operating Officer (Joe) to suggest that there might be a good reason to put the steering wheels of exports to Japan on the right-hand side of the car:

Marketing VP: . . . and so, gentlemen, since the Japanese drive—

CEO: Which reminds me, Joe, have you exercised those stock options yet?

Marketing VP: —on the left-hand side of—

COO: No, I thought I'd try to push those into the '87 tax year.

Marketing VP: —the road, maybe it'd be a good idea for the cars we're trying to sell over there—

CEO: But '87 is when we're going to have to declare the big incentive bonuses.

Marketing VP: —we should think about putting the steering wheel on—

COO: My accountant says we can have those paid into a family trust.

CEO: Is that right? Great. I'll call my man now. Ralph, good report. Come in anytime.

And then, in Tokyo, George Bush, who was apparently suffering from intestinal flu, provided a metaphor of his own for the entire operation:

HOW PRESIDENTS ARE REMEMBERED

At Valley Forge, our George would not give in.
Then Jefferson proclaimed the rights of man.
Abe Lincoln saved the Union for us all.
And Bush-san flashed his groceries in Japan.

Did it occur to me that there was something unfair in making fun of a President who, through no fault of his own, happened to be taken ill while on a foreign trip and nevertheless tried his best to carry on with his duties? Yes, it occurred to me.

15. *Republicans Scrambling*

The unfortunate episode in Japan, with the accompanying speculation about George Bush's health, revived talk about whether it might be wise to drop Dan Quayle from the 1992 ticket. Despite some revisionist surgery done on Quayle in a widely noted *Washington Post* series, polls showed that most Americans did not think that he was up to being President. For me, the re-evaluation of Quayle in the *Post* had turned out to be a personal vindication. In 1988 my suggestion that we pass a constitutional amendment making a C average a requirement for the presidency was widely viewed as a veiled attack on Dan Quayle. In response I pointed out that the amendment I had proposed— what would have been the Twenty-seventh Amendment to the Constitution—mentioned no names. It said, in its entirety: "No person shall be eligible for the Office of President who has not maintained a C average in any institution of higher education that such person attended, including institutions that such person bought his way into." The authors of the revisionist series in *The Washington Post*, David Broder and Bob Woodward, received permission to ask officials at DePauw University about Quayle's grade average, and they were told that it was a 2.1. In other words, if my amendment passed, Dan Quayle would fulfill the grade-average requirement for the presidency. You couldn't say that someone with a 2.1 had sailed over the Twenty-seventh Amendment bar without bothering to take off his sweatsuit, but you would have to say that he fulfilled the requirement.

DINGBAT RE-EVALUATED

The Post *now says, in contrast to the portraits*
    painting Quayle as hopeless joker,
He's fully mediocre.

He is, they say, without a doubt much smarter
    than the average Irish setter.
This makes me feel much better.

From the beginning of 1992, the press assumed that anything President Bush did, concerning Dan Quayle or anything else, was being done with a quick glance over the right shoulder at Pat Buchanan, who had audaciously decided to challenge an incumbent President of his own party. Even after

being attacked as an anti-Semite and a bully boy—
or, some would have said, because of being attacked
as an anti-Semite and a bully boy—Buchanan appeared to have a long-shot chance of gathering together the forces of the right that had always
suspected George Bush of not being a true believer:

WHAT BUCHANAN IS SAYING

*I'll say the things you really think—just try
  me.
Conservatives who loathe this Bush all buy me.
Complaints that I'm a bigot mystify me.
I'm not like Duke, whose thoughts and past are
  slimy.
In point of fact, no true-born Yanks decry me.
No, those opposed are all, by chance, named
  Hymie.*

When John Frohnmayer was fired as the chairman
of the National Endowment for the Arts, for instance, it was assumed that he had been a victim
of the 1992 challenge from the right:

PREVAILING PRESIDENTIAL
STANDARDS

*The head of the Endowment had to go.
The grants he gave, supposedly for arts,
Included some performances in which
Some scruffy folks exposed their private parts.*

The President abhors this dreadful smut.
He's saying so in every nook and cranny.
Unless, of course, Buchanan leaves the race,
In which case it's okay to show your fanny.

Everything the President did had a campaign echo—even if the echo was from a previous campaign:

GEORGE BUSH AT THE MARTIN LUTHER KING, JR., CENTER FOR NON-VIOLENT SOCIAL CHANGE, JANUARY 17, 1992

A splendid service held for King.
So nice of Bush to undertake it.
A pity, everybody said,
That Willie Horton couldn't make it.

Bush himself said he was itching to get into his campaign mode. He seemed to be reassembling the regular-guys language and down-home Texas customs that were familiar from the 1988 campaign. After he was installed in the White House, all of that had been more or less forgotten. He had reverted to someone whose wide-ranging experience had never touched his boarding-school WASP core—someone who had moved through life encased in a sort of tweedy cocoon. But the campaign mode was something different—or, as the campaigning George Bush would put it, somethin' difernt. I could imagine him rustling around in the back of the pantry for a package of pork rinds, and then going to the bedroom closet, where a pair of perfectly creased blue jeans had been hanging since 1988. I could hear him ordering the household staff to have a gun rack installed on his golf cart.

TEXAS REMAKE FOR THE CAMPAIGN

He puts aside his Mister Rogers voice,
And tries to ape the other Rogers (Kenny).
He drops his g's, and talks of "bidness," folks—
Except right now, alas, there isn't any.

At the beginning of 1992, Bush seemed so frenetic on the campaign stump that rumors began to circulate about the possibility that medicine he had been taking for his thyroid problem was causing manic episodes—rumors that, in turn, stirred up talk about whether a 2.1 was a good enough average for the presidency after all. On the campaign trail in New Hampshire, when Bush seemed to be enjoying himself the most, the audience seemed to be enjoying itself the least. Naturally, I was willing to offer some advice:

SOME ADVICE FOR THE PRESIDENT

It always seemed to me to be essential
For Presidents to act, well, presidential—

As Reagan did, with style I'm not pooh-
   poohing,
Though acting was, in fact, what he was doing.
But Bush, especially when he thinks he's
   trailing,
Believes plain folks respond to hyperflailing.
I think that he'd be likelier to woo us
By being more like Ron, not Jerry Lewis.

16. *The Primaries in Verse*

A deadline poet was at a disadvantage in commenting on the competition in the primaries for the Democratic presidential nomination: the two key words were "presumptive" and "vulnerable," both killers to rhyme. Even before Clinton had entered a primary—and even after he had failed to win the first few he entered—he was being described as the "presumptive candidate." Every time I saw that phrase, I imagined a representative of the party professionals and the press—an intrepid-looking explorer who's done up in a bush jacket and a pith helmet—trekking across the wilds of Arkansas. Finally, he comes upon the governor's mansion and says to the portly young man who answers the door, "The candidate, I presume." The questions raised in the early primaries about Clinton's character made Democrats fearful that they were in danger of nominating someone who'd be "vulnerable" to the Republican attack dogs in the general election campaign. After that, what the Democratic primary campaign was actually about was whether any way could be found to avoid nominating Clinton.

As Clinton's delegate count mounted, the campaigns of his surviving competitors sooner or later had to be based on telling the voters why Clinton was vulnerable. Jerry Brown took to that task with such relish that the Democratic Party finally asked him to cool it. Even Paul Tsongas, who had run a campaign so high-minded that its slogan was an entire book, began to talk about Clinton's "vulnerabilities of character and judgment." As spring faded into summer, Clinton became both more presumptive and more vulnerable all the time. George Bush—contemplating an approval rating that had dropped forty-five points since his Gulf glory days, wrestling with a recession that seemed stubbornly unyielding to his clothing purchases, listening to complaints that his campaign was being run by amateurs—could cheer himself up by looking at the Democratic Party's primaries:

THE NEW JERRY BROWN

When he was young, and serving St. Ignatius,
He was, by his vocation, kindly, gracious.
Converting at the speed of MS-DOS,
Embracing every sort of mishegoss,

*He still stayed kind. When he campaigned for
  guv*
Republicans were worthy of his love.
*All human beings were blessed, not just
  condoned.*
*These hippies can be sweet, when they're not
  stoned.*
Why, even as a party boss, I'd bet
He sweetly stroked the fattest cats, and yet
In this campaign, this sordid travelogue,
He now acts meaner than a junkyard dog.
He wasn't mean while curled up like a lotus—
Or straightened up it's easier to notice.

INSURMOUNTABLE OBSTACLE

I begged this Tsongas, "Get another vowel!"
Two consonants together, cheek by jowl,
Just feed the voters more than they can chew.
Another pol campaigning for the Senate—
Mrazek—bombed, confirming this same tenet.
He needed, too, a, e, i, o, or u.

Divorce is now no sin. We let that pass.
And younger pols admit to smoking grass.
In fact, confession's now a good maneuver.
But those with missing vowels cannot run.
A man named Rsevelt could not have won,
Unless he faced a man named Herbert Hver.

COMFORTING THOUGHTS FOR BUSH CAMPAIGN WORKERS RE QUESTIONS ON PERSONAL LIFE

We're lucky that our guy won't fall apart
If asked the question asked of Gary Hart.
(We're certain he is simply much too nice
To have some tweedy version of Ms. Rice.)
We know for certain he has never rolled
A cigarette of substances controlled
By law. He pops naught frowned on by the
  fuzz.
But, then, how come he talks the way he does?

THE VOTERS' MOOD AFTER THREE MONTHS OF INTENSE EXPOSURE TO THE DEMOCRATIC PROCESS

Some hero, star, or business whiz—
It doesn't matter who he is.
Just bring us someone we don't know.
We'd even try this Ross Perot.
You know a woman? Fine. Just get her.
The less we know of her the better.
We needn't hear their every sin—
The lies they've told, the times they've been
Upended by their own petards.
Just flip a coin, or cut the cards.

THE PRIMARIES ARE OVER

They're through.
It seems so long since Douglas Wilder blew
Through town, so long since Tsongas shrank,
 then grew,
So long since Harkin said, "So long. Adieu."

They're done.
And no one I know really had much fun—
Not even all the pols who didn't run,
And must have thought, "My God! I could
 have won!"

It's set,
Without my even having won a bet.
They're through. And that, my friends, I don't
 regret—
Except what follows may be grimmer yet.

17. Ross

Ross Perot was, of course, made for a deadline poet. Not his policies necessarily—his name. He presented to the world a crisp, two-syllable surname, accented on the second syllable for iambic pentameter convenience and ending with the sound of a long *o*—the vowel of a million rhymes. That was almost enough for my vote right there. Then there was his first name, a neat one syllable that was also an easy rhyme. The combination came out in ready-made meter. Consider this name compared to Michael Dukakis. Consider this name as contemplated by someone who, when shove came to push, had thought of only one rhyme for Bush.

Early in the campaign, it was revealed that before Ross left Texarkana for the Naval Academy, the family name had always been pronounced PEE-row. This revelation might have caused a moment or two of embarrassment. Perot was admired, after all, as a plain man of the people who would show no patience with the sort of fancy-pants Washington lobbyists who wore tassels on their shoes. He presented himself as the sort of man who would have little tolerance for upgrading the pronunciation of a family name so it sounded almost Continental, as if there might be a branch in Cap d'Antibes that still spells its name Pereaux, which rhymes with Bordeaux, which is what they like to drink if it's a decent vintage. Some Perot supporters might have been disillusioned to learn that before this family got rich it was happy enough to call itself PEE-row, which sounds like the name of a family that never heard of Cap d'Antibes or Bordeaux or any other place outside of pickup range of Texarkana, Texas, and never drinks anything that doesn't come in a long-necked bottle. When I pronounce the name PEE-row out loud, I can almost hear some sheriff saying to his deputy, "You better check out the Dew Drop Inn when you're out that way, Hiram. I hear a bunch of them PEE-rows are hanging out there, and you know that always means trouble before the evening's over."

There could have been no such grumbling among deadline poets. As Ross himself might have put it, the name PEE-row doesn't rhyme with diddly-squat, except maybe Nero. I could only be grateful for the change to puh-ROW. I welcomed Ross Perot to the race, even though he didn't seem to have any idea in which direction he was going to take the country once he got under the hood and got its spark plugs all squeaky clean:

PEROT BEGINS

Your flow, Perot, of cash—your dough—
Is surely part of your appeal.
Your campaign pro will crow, Perot:
"At least this guy's too rich to steal."

A can-do Joe, gung-ho, Perot,
You find the White House worth pursuing.
But whoa, Perot. You need to show
That what you'll do is what needs doing.

So nu, Perue? We're asking you
Your plans, your thoughts, your hopes, your
* fears.*
There's not a clue. What would you do?
So speak. We are (like you) all ears.

In campaign interviews, Perot turned out to be unconventional—combative, insistent about being the sort of person who would rather get things done than talk about them, disdainful of the sort of politician who tried to waffle when asked a direct question. Perot never waffled. He gave direct, straight-from-the-shoulder answers—although, as

reporters started digging, it turned out that some
of the answers were not true.

THE ROSS PEROT GUIDE TO ANSWERING EMBARRASSING QUESTIONS

When something in my history is found
That contradicts the views I now propound,
Or shows that I am surely hardly who
I claim to be, here's what I usually do:

I lie.
I simply, baldly falsify.
I look the fellow in the eye,
And cross my heart and hope to die—
And lie.

I don't apologize. Not me. Instead,
I say I never said the things I said.
Nor did the things that people saw me do.
Confronted with some things they know *are*
*   true,*

I lie.
I offer them no alibi,
Nor say, "You oversimplify."
I just deny, deny, deny.
I lie.

I hate the weasel words some slickies use
To blur their pasts or muddy up their views.
Not me. I'm blunt. One thing that makes me
  great
Is that I'll never dodge or obfuscate.

I'll lie.

A couple of weeks after that poem was published, I got a call from the wily and parsimonious Victor S. Navasky, who proudly informed me that Pete Seeger, the folk singer, had set the words of "The Ross Perot Guide to Answering Embarrassing Questions" to music and had been singing the resulting song at rallies and concerts.

"I don't suppose the people's troubadour troubles himself with such bourgeois fripperies as permissions or copyrights," I said to Navasky.

Secretly, though, I was pleased. I was a lyricist again—a role I hadn't played since the filming of *If There's No Nova Scotia in Nova Scotia, There Can't Be Any French Fries in France*. When Seeger himself telephoned, I told him that I was delighted to have him use the poem. He was phoning, in fact, to say that he needed a couple of more verses to flesh out the song. I turned them out that week. One was about the rule in Perot's company banning beards—a rule whose existence he had flatly denied until some reporter produced a court case and a company book of regulations—and the other was about the old charge that he liked to hire private investigators to poke around in the lives of people who had crossed him:

> They ask if as a boss I found it weird
> For men to wear a mustache or a beard,
> And ruled that personnel would give the boot
> To anyone found facially hirsute.

> I lie.
> I simply, baldly falsify.
> I look the fellow in the eye,
> And cross my heart and hope to die—
> And lie.

> On TV shows I'm often asked to state
> If I have gumshoes who'll investigate
> A citizen I think has done me wrong.
> I bristle, then I try the same old song:

> I lie.
> I offer them no alibi,
> Nor say, "You oversimplify."
> I just deny, deny, deny.
> I lie.

A couple of weeks after that, Ross Perot suddenly withdrew from the race.

PEROT ENDS

Some said, in tears, "Oh, please don't go,
*   Perot.*
You'd make this country once again sublime."
They said, in tears, "Don't go, Perot, we know
Just you could make the trains all run on
*   time."*

And some, in anger, said, "This schmo, Perot,
Assured us he was tough, the problems dinky.
We should have seen that soon Perot would
*   show*
That underneath he's softer than a Twinkie."

For you, H. Ross Perot, the cock did crow.
And we were left one saying from the bosses:
"When rows get tough to hoe, the tough just
*   blow,*
Because the bottom line is Cut your losses."

Had Seeger and I driven him out? We might have
been willing to take credit for it, except that a couple
of months later he was back in the race anyway.
The conventional wisdom was that *Newsweek* had
brought him back by emblazoning the word "quit-
ter" above his name on its cover the week after he
dropped out; CW, as *Newsweek* itself likes to call
it, held that Perot had returned because he couldn't
stand the thought of that word being in the first

paragraph of his obituary someday. I felt obligated
to write a churlish poem about his return:

ON THE REAPPEARANCE OF
ROSS PEROT

The show, Perot,
Has closed. You quit. And those, Perot, are
    facts.
You know, Perot,
This is the place that has no second acts.

So go, Perot.
Just leave us now. Please go, and take your
    baggage.
No mo', Perot,
Do not repeat on us like last night's cabbage.

On the other hand, I might as well acknowledge
that part of me was just happy to have that rhyme
back.

18. *Multilingualism*

So far, scholars have ignored the entire subject of multilingualism among deadline poets. I can't blame them. It's a real can of worms. Light-verse writers in America, like subdivision developers in Southern California, customarily toss in a little Spanish now and then; Spanish is, after all, a language with cooperative vowel sounds. Nobody questions the rhyming of "say so" with "*chile con queso.*" Although French verb sounds have to be nudged along a bit, the use of both French and English is appropriate when commenting on Canada, a country that is officially bilingual. What is appropriate when commenting on Canada is not something that most American commentators have to concern themselves with, but I have certain responsibilities in that area: I happen to hold the record for number of consecutive columns by an American on a Canadian subject (two). I may also be the only poet in history to have written a poem about the Meech Lake Accord, a constitutional agreement that some saw as the last opportunity to keep Francophone Quebec from seceding. At the time—the summer of 1990—the Meech Lake Accord had just fallen two short of winning the unanimous confirmation from provincial parliaments that it required, partly because of the efforts of a single Cree legislator in Manitoba. A number of Francophones had said that its defeat was the last straw. Quebec, they said, would surely secede from the Canadian confederation:

A BILINGUAL CONVERSATION
(After the Meech Lake Accord Failed to Pass the Newfoundland and Manitoba Parliaments)

"A pity! But I'm sure we all agree:
We'll wait two years, then make another plea."

"Finis."

"I know Meech Lake's defeat has caused a stir.
What can one say, except 'Such things occur'?"

"A toute à l'heure."

"But most of us were pro—believe you me.
Why, just because the Newfies and one Cree
Have not allowed this noble pact to be
You can't intend to pack your bags and flee."

"Mais oui."

"*And how about bilingual goals declared?*
And how about the Anglophones who cared?
What say you to the history we've shared?"

"Merde."

Quebec stuck around for the moment, and I became accustomed to using French in poems that were not about Canada. You might say that a bit of French added a certain *je ne sais quoi*. You might say that I was running out of rhymes in English. I did a poem, for instance, about how expensive Europe had become because of the weak dollar:

WEAK DOLLAR BLUES

I got them finally got to Paris and the dollar is
*   dropping blues.*
I go to all the chic shops, but all I can do is
*   peruse.*
There're clothes here that I'd like to hoard,
But a Coke costs as much as a Ford.
I don't know who's to blame, but whoever it is,
*   well, j'accuse.*
I got them finally got to Paris and the dollar is
*   dropping blues.*

And a poem about a narrow win for the pro-Europe forces in a French vote on the European Community:

ON THE EUROPEAN TREATY VOTE

Supporters of the treaty vote in France
Now say "It's oui*!" "We've won the day!" et*
    cetera.
The numbers, though, do not a landslide make.
It's not exactly oui, *but more* peut-êtera.

The foreign language I have most often reached for in poetry, though, is not French but Yiddish. I can't say that this is part of any particular tradition in English-language poetry. As far as I've been able to ascertain, for instance, Wordsworth knew no Yiddish at all, although he may have once referred to his publisher as a *gonif.* Yiddish lingers in the reserve vocabulary of anyone who lives in New York, and these days, even as intellectuals write essays lamenting the evidence that Yiddish as a spoken and written language is dying, television comedy has spread bite-sized Yiddishisms across the country. I was startled to learn, through the always reliable medium of a television commercial, that one version of country line dancing—country line dancing!—is called the tush-push. (Yes, that does reveal one more rhyme for Bush, but it's one I avoided out of respect.)

A lot of New Yorkers, regardless of ethnic background, might say *gonif* when they want to say "thief" and *tsouris* when they want to say "troubles" and *bubbe* when they want to say "grandma" and *schnook* when they want to say "jerk." These days, of course, a subway passenger overheard talking about his grandfather is much more likely to say *abuelo* than *zayde*; if there is an announcement that a stalled train ahead is causing a delay of unknown duration, he's more likely to say *caramba* than *oy vay*. Yiddish newspapers have given way to newspapers in Spanish and Chinese and Russian and Greek. But Yiddish remains the language of New York contention. I once proposed that people arriving from other parts of the country be given an English-Yiddish phrase book when they got off the bus. The phrases would not be phrases like "Could you please direct me to the nearest post office?" but phrases like "May boils erupt on your liver and spleen!" Yiddish popped up even in a poem I wrote about Princess Di, when her eating problems and marital difficulties seemed to dominate the American press:

THE TROUBLES OF PRINCESS DI

Oh, Di, we sigh, as tabloids pry and spy.
(They're certain there's no way this stuff could
   bore us.)

> *Malwed, it's said, you keep yourself unfed.*
> *So young to have such monumental tsouris!*
>
> *They're sly. They lie. They try to classify*
> *Travails with every word in the thesaurus.*
> *Forsooth, our sighs are based upon your*
>   *youth:*
> *How many years of this now lie before us?*

And again when, as the former Yugoslavia began to
break up, Croatia, once known for its enthusiastic
collaboration with Nazi Germany, seemed to be the
victim, as a particularly thuggish Serbia warmed up
for a go at the Bosnian Muslims:

THE NEW WORLD ORDER— CENTRAL EUROPEAN DIVISION

> *Croatians are the good guys now,*
> *Although their past is slightly shady:*
> *So worry not that these same guys*
> *Chased both your* bubbe *and your* zayde.

But all of that was only bilingualism. Multilingualism did not come to my poetry until years
later, when I wrote a two-line poem about Lloyd
Bentsen that included three languages—English,
Latin, and Texan:

A SHORT HISTORY OF
LLOYD BENTSEN'S DEALINGS WITH
SPECIAL INTERESTS

The man is known for quo pro quidness.
In Texas, that's how folks do bidness.

19. Getting into the Ring

The general election campaign had basically been on since Buchanan faltered and Clinton emerged triumphant from the New York primary. Any doubts about that were erased by the White House response to the disturbances in south central Los Angeles. Before the disturbances, the Bush Administration had a clear and unequivocal policy concerning the difficulty that American cities found themselves in: Don't talk about it. Jack Kemp, the one member of the cabinet who had shown any interest in discussing such issues, was considered to have approximately as much clout in the White House as the ambassador from Burkina Faso. Then came the Los Angeles riots, and a lot of attention on what the urban policy of the Bush Administration was—or, as some would have put it, if it was. Jack Kemp found himself with a pocketful of Air Force One matchbooks:

JACK KEMP (A WHITE GUY'S RAP)

APRIL

Jack is dissed by Bush's troops.
Jack's cut out of all the loops.
White House dudes say Jack's a pain:
Jack can't tell which stream is main.
Jack still talks of urban blight.
Jack forgot the votes are white.
When the White House has a do,
Jack's as welcome as the flu.

MAY

White House dudes say, "Jack's our man.
We're behind Jack's housing plan.
Jack's the greatest. Jack's the top.
Jack's our favorite photo op.
Urban program? There's no lack
(Get the details there from Jack).
Jack's the coolest of them all.
We're with Jack, at least till fall."

In the lull between the selection of the nominees and the conventions that ostensibly exist for the selection of the nominees, "vulnerable" was becoming a word used to describe not just Bill Clinton but also George Bush. Looking back, I'd say it was a feeling that had been slowly growing since Harris Wofford cleaned Dick Thornburgh's clock in Pennsylvania. A lot of commentators traced Bush's problem to his inability to communicate concern about the economy, and a lot of commentators believed the problem had begun long before that—when he broke his promise not to raise taxes. All Presidents break promises, of course, but no President had set himself up for the fall as dramatically as Bush, who said at the 1988 Republican National Convention that he would respond to Democratic pressure to raise taxes by saying, "Read my lips: No new taxes." Peggy Noonan, known to all as the Republicans' smartest speechwriter, had managed to reserve the most unforgettable phrase in the speech for a promise that Bush would, sooner or later, probably have to hope that everybody had forgotten.

For the Republicans, it was one of a series of dumb moves, all pushed by people known to be particularly brilliant. When it came time to break the read-my-lips pledge, for instance, Bush was apparently assured by the smartest of the smart, Richard Darman, that nobody would care, since politicians break promises all the time. Darman's partner in the negotiation that led to the promise breaking was, of course, John Sununu, a White House disaster best described by another Republican, Ed Rollins, as a lesson in the perils of telling your child that he has a high IQ. After a while, it began to occur to me that the dumbest moves in a campaign are often made by people who have reputations for being exceedingly smart—a theory that seemed to be confirmed by the behavior of William Kristol, who was often called the smartest person in the White House.

As Dan Quayle's chief of staff, Kristol pushed the family-values agenda, a dead end that stalled the Republican campaign for a month. He was the leading hawk in the war against Murphy Brown. What could be dumber than attacking a fictional character—someone who could say absolutely anything and would always have the last word? The answer: attacking a widely adored fictional character. You'd think the Republicans had learned that lesson after Bush said that American families needed to be more like the Waltons and less like the Simpsons—to which Bart Simpson had replied, on the air, "Hey, we're just like the Waltons: both families spend a lot of time praying for the end of the Depression." But Quayle lit into Murphy Brown for having a baby out of wedlock. He told us how important it was to have a father around. Nobody could argue with that, although it called to mind how important Quayle's own father, an early member of the John Birch Society and a man of some influence at DePauw, had been in his son's life:

A FATHER'S ROLE

A father plays a role, says Quayle.
It's true. He surely should acknowledge
His own dear dad, who, first of all,
Was there to buy him into college.

And teach him John Birch songs and stuff
That Dad and Dan sang by the hour—
Sad songs of how the Commies plant
Such spies as Dwight D. Eisenhower.

And teach him golf—yes, how to face
The terrors of the links unblinking,
At clubs designed to guard against
The threat of blacks and Jews and thinking.

It's good that Dad could pull some strings
And had the clout to settle whether
Young Dan would go to Vietnam.
'Cause families should stay together.

Although it seemed difficult to believe later, there was a time there, early in the summer of 1992, when Bill Clinton faded from the pages of newspapers. Presumably the Clinton campaign was madly refining policy positions and hairdos, but as far as the public was able to tell, Clinton had all but disappeared:

WHATEVER HAPPENED TO CLINTON?

Whatever happened to Clinton?
What do you hear from young Bill?
Is he in witness protection?
Could he have skipped to Brazil?

We in the press really miss him.
Let's hope that soon he'll be found.
Now that we've tired of Ross, we
Need Bill for kicking around.

Then came the Democratic National Convention in New York, and he was back, joined by Al Gore, another Southern moderate who liked to distinguish himself from the old-fashioned Democratic liberals. The combination turned out to be more than the sum of its parts. Democrats seemed buoyed by the sight of two energetic, up-to-date young men talking about change—although my Aunt Rosie said, "If those young men don't watch it, their weight is going to get away from them." I had to contemplate the possibility that the Republicans might be tempted to refer to the Democratic ticket as the Blubber Bubbas ("Are men who order the cottage-cheese-and-fruit-salad and then pick at a companion's double order of cheese french fries to the point at which the plate requires no washing really who you want making life-and-death decisions for this nation?"). Suddenly the Democrats were cheering, and I, trying to get in the spirit of things, composed a cheer:

CLINTON AND GORE:
A CHEER FOR MODERATES

Clinton and Gore, Clinton and Gore—
Both of them born since the war!

They're not liberals, like before—
Technocratic to the core.
Clinton and Gore, Clinton and Gore!

We have got the nominees.
You should see their SATs!

Clinton and Gore, Clinton and Gore—
Glamour smoothies we adore,
Middle-class forevermore.
Once again, that mighty roar:
Clinton and Gore, Clinton and Gore.

Baby boomers, baby boomers, yes, yes, yes.
Both these guys know how to dress.

Yeaaaa, team!

In response to this threat, George Bush finally did what he had apparently been hoping to avoid even as criticism of the Republican campaign mounted—he turned to his old friend James Baker, known to some as the Houston Smoothie. Baker, who in 1988 had managed to receive credit for the Republican campaign's triumph without receiving blame for its sleaziness, reluctantly left the post of Secretary of State to take over a campaign that some thought only he could save:

BAKER, BAKER, MIRACLE MAKER
(A Campaign Nursery Rhyme)

Baker, Baker, miracle maker,
What will your miracle be?
Some Hillary trashing?
A bout of gay-bashing?
A shot of Gore hugging a tree?

Baker, Baker, miracle maker,
Your statesmanship always assures
That dirty stuff's done
By some hired Hun.
The dirt sticks on his hands, not yours.

20. *General Election*

What even Baker couldn't get around was the recession. In American politics, a weak economy is traditionally blamed on the President, whether he had a lot to do with causing it or not; the model is blaming a losing football season on the coach. The Republicans apparently thought they could get through the campaign with personal attacks on Bill Clinton, a man who, to put it as kindly as possible, seemed blessed with at least his share of human frailties. In the spirit of having called Michael Dukakis a "card-carrying member of the American Civil Liberties Union," Bush painted Clinton's student trip to Moscow as a sinister event—leaving open the possibility that young Bill had been recruited by the KGB to act as its agent-in-place in Fayetteville. But nobody seemed interested. Even reminders of Clinton's efforts to avoid military service during the Vietnam War seemed to have limited impact:

A REPUBLICAN CANVASSER DISCUSSES CLINTON'S DRAFT PROBLEMS WITH A PROSPECTIVE VOTER

"Young Willie Clinton did not go."
    "That's so. I know, I know. It's so."
"And now he can't remember why."
    "That's true. He has no alibi."
"At least four versions have been heard."
    "Yes, doubts exist about his word."
"Then you're for us? Oh, what a thrill!"
    "Well, sorry, no. I'll stick with Bill."
"But aren't you shocked? Dismayed?
  Annoyed?"
        "Yes, all of those: I'm unemployed."

Any discussion of Clinton's alleged misdeeds was also undercut by persistent rumors that Bush had known more about the Iran-Contra dealings than he had been willing to admit:

BUSH AND IRAN-CONTRA

I

He wasn't one who sought to dupe
The public. Members of that group
Made sure he wasn't in the loop.
They kept from him the straightest poop.

A gentleman must never snoop.
He knew no more than Betty Boop.

II
Or else, I fear, he's in the soup.

In search of dirt on Clinton, a Republican political appointee in the State Department, Elizabeth Tamposi, looked through his supposedly private passport file. It was the sort of sharpened-spikes campaigning that had been blamed on Lee Atwater rather than James Baker in 1988, and some seemed content to do the same in 1992, overlooking the awkward detail that Lee Atwater had died a couple of years before. The file search went beyond Clinton himself:

Yes, State did rifle Clinton's file,
To try to smear him as a Commie.
And when they came up short on that,
They tried the file of Clinton's mommy.

That's right: they actually went through the passport file of Clinton's mother—a cheerful Hot Springs horseplayer who seemed unlikely to have traveled to a Communist country, since the Reds were always notorious in certain circles for a philosophical aversion to racetracks. Mom was clean. Bashing Hillary without offending working women had turned out to be trickier than predicted. The economy remained in the tank. People who knew

James Baker's tendency over the years to put a lot of distance between himself and any disaster began to comment on the fact that the nominal head of the White House operation—the indispensable man who was to save the Bush campaign—was almost never seen in public.

BAKER, BAKER, MIRACLE MAKER
(Reprise)

Baker, Baker, miracle maker,
Where did your miracle go?
The gay-bashing flopped,
The Red scare was dropped.
What more do you have from below?

Baker, Baker, miracle maker,
No wonder you haven't been seen.
In this sort of fight
One stays out of sight.
A gentleman's hands remain clean.

For once, the prognostications were on the money. In the last week of the campaign, Bush seemed for a moment to be closing the gap. But then the Bush momentum was blunted by a couple of jolts—one from Bush himself and one from Lawrence Walsh, the Iran-Contra special prosecutor, who had been bitterly attacked by the Republicans for months. Bush, calling his opponents "bozos," began flailing about in a campaign mode reminiscent of not just Jerry Lewis but Jerry Lewis in those later movies that even Dean Martin didn't think were funny. Lawrence Walsh, in the course of adding some indictments to the case he was trying to make against Caspar Weinberger, released a document that specifically contradicted Bush's longtime claim to having been out of the loop. The damage done by Walsh's timing, some thought, was a confirmation of one of life's lessons that George Bush's mother had presumably tried to teach him: Those who don't treat the help with some respect may live to regret it.

On election night there was a lot of talk about how the generation that had fought the Second World War had passed the torch on to the baby boomers. The television picture that summed up the generational change for me was Bill Clinton and Al Gore hugging each other. Not just clapping each other on the back—hugging! Is it possible to imagine Dwight D. Eisenhower in a long hug? Can we contemplate Richard Nixon and Spiro Agnew hugging, with Nixon's arms jerking away from Agnew's back every now and then to flash the victory sign above them? Congratulations came in from all over the world, and on behalf of my colleagues of the press, I added my little tip of the hat:

TO BILL CLINTON—
A WORD OF WARNING

At last, the prize is yours, and you may guess
That what we wrote—we jackals of the press—
About the other side is indication
Of sympathy toward your Administration.
Not so. We liked to knock poor Bush about
'Cause he was in. (We are, by nature, out.)
So we see not a knight upon a charger
But just a target—large and growing larger.
The very ones you think you ought to thank'll
Now turn around and bite you in the ankle.

21. A Trio of Bittersweet Poems of Farewell

ADIEU, BUSH'S MEN

The bell for Bush's men now slowly knells.
The cabinet is saying its farewells.
(So many hope that they can safely mosey
Before the testimony of Tamposi
Reveals just who fed what into the shredder
On whether Bill was Red and his mom
*   Redder.)*
We say, observing as the Feds unhitch
These guys so gray we don't know which is
*   which*
And they join corporate boards or institutes,
Goodbye to all you Protestants in suits.

ADIEU TO YOU, J. DANFORTH QUAYLE

Adieu to you, J. Danforth Quayle,
As off upon life's sea you sail.
For some of us, real tears are welling.
We'll miss those goofs, that stare, your
  spelling.
We'll miss you, Dan, until we've found
Some other soul to kick around.

But hark! Is someone at the door?
Why, yes. Come in. Well, Albert Gore . . .

ADIEU, GEORGE BUSH

Farewell to you, George Herbert Walker.
Though never treasured as a talker—
Your predicates were often prone
To wander, nounless, off alone—
You did your best in your own way,
The way of Greenwich Country Day.
We wish you well. Just take your ease,
And never order Japanese.
May your repose remain unblighted—
Unless of course you get indicted.

22. *Transition*

On one level, the press was in complete agreement with Bill Clinton: we agreed that it was good to have a change. As we emerged on the other side of the Bush gray-out, a sea of fresh new ankles had been exposed for us to snap at. We even had questions about whether the sort of change Clinton had promised was, in fact, taking place: If a rejection of the old, corrupt, Washington way of doing things was what the election was about, why were all these Washington lawyers and lobbyists gathering around the new President? Why were so many of them involved in decisions about who would get jobs?

SO FAR

So far, young Bill's done very well—
Articulate, uncowed by hassles.
His staff is young and fresh and bright.

In Little Rock, they've gathered passels
Of whizzes set to re-create
Jack's Camelot, including castles.
A sage, though, from the shadows warns,
"Beware of friends whose shoes have tassels."

CLARKCLIFFORD
(A Cautionary Air, Sung to the Tune of
"Titwillow")

As lawyers whose clients need government clout
Clarkclifford, Clarkclifford, Clarkclifford
Decide who'll be in and decide who'll be out
Clarkclifford, Clarkclifford, Clarkclifford
We grumble, says Clinton, much more than we
   should:
No conflicts can happen, it's all understood
That these are his friends and they've come to do
   good.
Clarkclifford, Clarkclifford, Clarkclifford

And if Clinton and Gore together spent the campaign displaying youthful energy, why was Gore standing silently behind Clinton at Little Rock press conferences? Had he become—to use an old Russian phrase once used about one of Gorbachev's vice presidents, Gennady Yanayev—a piano in the shrubbery?

OBSERVATION AT A CLINTON PRESS CONFERENCE

What's that, behind the President-elect—
That man-like object stiff from head to toe?
A statue of a noble Southern pol?
A waxen image crafted by Tussaud?
But wait! He breathed. He blinked. He
*   scratched his nose.*
This couldn't be an adamantine blob.
This man-like object seems to be alive.
It's Albert Gore. He's there to do his job.

And if Hillary Clinton had competed in cookie-baking contests during the campaign, how come she was suddenly going by the name of Hillary Rodham Clinton?

THE FINAL SHOCKER

Well, Watergate seems puny when compared
To this, the latest shocker that's been bared—
A tempest worse by far than Teapot Dome
Or orgies in the final days of Rome
Or Black Sox games that turned out to be
*   phony*
Or fair Godiva starkers on her pony.
More shocking than the stuff they did in
*   Sodom?*
Yes, Hillary's gone back to using Rodham.

And if these guys were so smart, why couldn't they find an Attorney General nominee?

THE BALLAD OF ZOE BAIRD
(May Stephen Sondheim find any resemblance to "The Ballad of Sweeney Todd" nearly coincidental)

Attend the tale of Zoe Baird,
And how her nomination fared.
She made no effort to evade
The fact she'd employed a Peruvian maid.
She'd done this deed to get au paired,
Had Zoe Baird,
A corporate lawyer in Hartford.

Transition said she'd be okay.
There'd be a minor fine to pay,
Some awkward moments to endure.
But quick confirmation was totally sure
For Zoe,
For Zoe Baird,
A corporate lawyer in Hartford.

"You can spill the beans, Zoe. Tell them what is
*   true,*
Even though in Washington we rarely do."

The senators were nice indeed.
They said she'd been a mom in need.
They didn't seem to care at all.

Then telephones started to ring off the wall.
And suddenly they all got scared
Of Zoe Baird,
A corporate lawyer in Hartford.

Suddenly shocked at what they saw,
They said that Zoe had broken the law.
This was a thing they couldn't condone,
Said some of those whose children were grown.
Public respect for the law would decrease,
Said some of those who'd voted for Meese.
Zoe withdrew, Zoe skedaddled.
Now pols with children at home are all rattled.
By Zoe,
By Zoe Baird,
A corporate lawyer in Hartford.

And if these guys were so clean, how come so much lobbyist money had been solicited to pay for the inauguration?

LINGERING REFLECTIONS ON A POPULIST INAUGURAL

The people's first hurrah was furnished free
By folks to whom some favors then accrue.
The people's President thinks that's okay.
He says that lobbyists are people, too.

And those were not the only questions we had.

WELCOME, PRESIDENT CLINTON

I

Before we even said congratulations,
You got attacked for waffling on the Haitians,
And waffling once again about Saddam—
A fellow we've elected you to bomb.
It's said the message your inaugural sent
Is government remains for sale, or rent.
On taxes and the deficit, it's said,
Your words and lips were easily misread.
You're now so much the figure that we pillory
We've nearly all forgotten about Hillary.
The public's mad. The press has formed a mob.

II

You're absolutely sure you want this job?

23. *Things Happen*

Would I be commenting on Amy Fisher? The Long Island episode involving Ms. Fisher and Joey Buttafuoco was so seamy that all three networks cranked up their automated sleaze extruders to deal with it in made-for-television movies. Was that the sort of subject that someone who hoped to become poet laureate should discuss? Would those British laureates who had traditionally written about royal birthdays and royal jubilees have dealt with such goings-on? The answer is less obvious than it once was: considering how the British royal family has been behaving in recent years, one of the surprising factors of the Amy Fisher scandal was that, as far as anyone has been able to ascertain, no members of the House of Windsor were involved. Still, when it comes to subject matter, poets have certain standards—although, I had to admit, I had done a poem on fish-smoking and on the sexual habits of the California mouse and was even then, as the play-by-play was coming in on the customary scandals of spring training, contemplating a poem for the opening of the baseball season:

BASEBALL'S BACK

Yes, baseball's back. Once more our sporting
*   passion'll*
Embrace this game, this hallowed pastime
*   national.*
We'll fill the stadium our taxes built
Because the owner threatened he would jilt
Our city, which might die, it was implied,
Without this centerpiece of civic pride.
We'll cheer our heroes when ahead or losing,
Forgetting tales of date rape, drugs, and
*   boozing.*
We'll cheer the way they hit and catch and
*   pitch.*
We'll cheer the agents who have made them
*   rich.*
So, greedy owners, pampered jocks, you all
Are welcomed once again. Okay, play ball!

Then one day, while reading a long story in one of the more respectable papers about the coverage of the Amy Fisher affair, I came to understand how scribblers of high station manage to discuss such events and retain respectability: the trick is to comment, at some length but with some disdain, on the excessiveness of the coverage:

CURSE

If someone needed to be cursed,
I know for sure what I would wish her:
Imprisonment where she could watch
Just films that deal with Amy Fisher.

The other device for trying to disguise a titillating story as something more substantial is, of course, to dress it up as a metaphor—in this case, a metaphor for the deterioration of the American suburban dream. Any number of articles said that Amy Fisher's story was a symbol of corrupt Long Island. An alternate theory was that corrupt Long Island was a symbol for corrupt every place else, since corruption was being revealed right and left throughout the entire world. In Japan, the party that had ruled for thirty-eight years was being brought down by revelations of payoff schemes slick enough to impress a Chicago alderman. As an anticorruption investigation picked up steam in Italy, just about everyone in public life there seemed to be either facing indictment or already safely in the slammer. There was even an accusation of a link between the Mafia and a former Prime Minister:

ON THE ACCUSATION THAT FORMER
ITALIAN PREMIER GIULIO ANDREOTTI
KISSED THE MAFIA'S BOSS OF BOSSES

Alas, poor Giulio Andreotti:
According to a source they've got, he
Showed himself to be the Mafia's pawn.
Though Giulio's colleagues can't be haughty—
For they themselves have been quite naughty—
Smooching with the don is still not on.

Who's kissing whom is not considered mere gossip if one of the people involved is a Mafia don and one a Prime Minister. In this country, the sort of shockers previously available only about people in show business were increasingly told about holders of high office—not only in newspapers but also in the modern version of biographies:

BIO DEGRADABLE

Biography once glorified the great—
The leaders we were meant to emulate.
But now a subject's warts are stressed a lot.
It sometimes seems that warts are all he's got.
A list of what we're told in books of late
Could cause some squeamish types to emigrate:
A witness says it truly was a shock
To see J. Edgar Hoover in a frock;
The Roosevelts had notions rather swanky

About the role of quiet hanky-panky;
John Kennedy's commitment to amour
Left precious little time for peace or war;
And L.B.J., when caught up in competing,
Could do some things that do not bear
    repeating.
There's only one exception to this mess.
It's Harry Truman (and "The Boss," his Bess).
With scholarship to come, this all could vary—
But not, I hope, the part about our Harry.

24. And Then

Clinton's promise to focus like a laser on the economy had political commentators worried: how were we going to discuss the President's new economic plan without revealing that we have no understanding of economics whatsoever?

In conversation I relied on the old method of devising one sentence that made me sound rather knowledgeable. Whenever the subject came up, I repeated the sentence in a confident tone of voice, even though I hadn't the slightest idea of what it meant. My sentence was: "The question is: What's going to happen when the deficit-reduction component begins to bite?"

This was a sentence I had cobbled together from a couple of different phrases I'd heard on the radio in a discussion between two economists who were both unintelligible in an impressive way. One expert said the key would be when something started to bite, although I didn't catch precisely what it was. For all I know, it might have been trout. The other expert mentioned the deficit-reduction component. I stuck the two phrases together. That opening—"The question is"—was my own little contribution.

I liked the result. It had a nice, authoritative ring to it. I've always thought that the word "component" alone could make you sound as if you knew what you were talking about, and this seemed to confirm that theory. For a while my sentence was very effective. People would say, "What do you think of the Clinton economic plan?"

"The question is: What's going to happen when the deficit-reduction component begins to bite?" I would say, in a voice that I hoped sounded like the voice of a tweedy man with a pipe.

"That's a good point," they'd say.

How was I able to get away with such blatant fakery? Simple: most of the people I talk to don't understand economics any better than I do.

Still, I was concerned. The economy presents a special problem for a deadline poet. There is no rhyme for deficit. There is no rhyme for stimulus. As it turned out, though, the Clinton Administration was not completely dominated by efforts to fix the economy. That was partly because so much was happening—most of it horrible—in places like Bosnia and Somalia. It was partly because Clinton's notion of concentration resembles a laser less than it does a MIRV missile—warheads going off everywhere, sometimes far from the target. As the Clintonists began tossing off plans on how to fix every part of the society, the overwhelming impression I got was that they all seemed so *busy*:

BUSY, BUSY, BUSY

The deficit may vanish without trace
Once Clinton's economic plan's in place.
A White House plan for health is on its way,
And plans (we think) for soldiers who are gay.
The White House has a plan for every ill
This country suffers from, or ever will:
A plan to vaccinate each child right now,
A plan to change each sword into a plow,
A service corps to stiffen up our youth,
A forest summit that will seek the truth
On whether too much weight has been allotted
To owls whose claim to fame is that they're
  spotted,
A plan to make the airbus obsolete,
A plan to change inspection rules for meat.
The multitude of plans has folks perplexed.
Are plans to change the weather coming next?

The attempt to solve the controversy over logging in the Pacific Northwest seemed almost a matter of Clinton's having a spare weekend on the way to a summit conference in Vancouver:

THE FOREST SUMMIT ISSUE

The issue's both acute and chronic.
It calls for wisdom Solomonic.
For some are said to be besotted
By owls whose wings and breasts are spotted.
And some would simply like releases
To slice these owls in tiny pieces
And serve them broiled or grilled or fried.
If I were told, "Okay, decide
The future of the spotted owl,"
I'd think of throwing in the towel.

And then Clinton discovered—and this seemed to surprise him—that there were people in Washington who opposed his policies. The gridlock that was supposed to evaporate with his election seemed to be generating as much honking and swearing as it had caused when the bus caught halfway through the intersection was being driven by George Bush. Senator Nunn said he was opposed to ending the military's ban on homosexuals. Senator Dole fought Clinton's economic plan without quarter. Congressman Dan Rostenkowski, who was supposed to be shepherding the Clinton economic package through the House, was having troubles of his own—leaks and hints that seemed to be pointing toward an eventual indictment having to do with some money drained from the House post office. I was able to devote a poem to each of these public servants

without having to worry about a rhyme for deficit
or stimulus:

THOUGHTS ON THE SENATOR FROM GEORGIA WHO MIGHT HAVE BEEN PRESIDENT

He doesn't draw the minicam.
He lacks, perhaps, a touch of ham.
He's charming as an angiogram,
Is Sam.

If he had run, he might have won,
Although his manner weighs a ton.
And we'd be having not much fun
With Nunn.

DOLE

Emerging in a new, more powerful role,
The senator from Kansas, Robert Dole,
Infuses now in everything he says
The juice of acting as the shadow Prez.
(And like the groundhog earlier this year,
He'd like to see that shadow disappear.)
In youth, Bob Dole was poor. He's not forgot
That some folks have, some other folks have
   not.

Compared with have-not life—a drudge, a
  debtor—
He seems to think that have's a whole lot
  better.
So now his wife, Elizabeth, and he
Are fixed among the rulers of D.C.
And Bob must muse, in voce *rather* sotto,
"Well, now, I don't think we're in Kansas,
  Toto."

ROSTENKOWSKI ACCUSED

Alas, oh woe, poor Chairman Rostenkowski—
Chicago pol writ large, and Clinton's Housekey
(The way to open doors up on the Hill).
The Feds imply his hand was in the till.
Some twenty grand, claim G-men counting
  beans,
Was nicked in stamps through special ways and
  means.
These facts, some say, would argue for
  acquittal:
Why would a pol so big steal sums so little?

And then Clinton discovered—and this seemed
to surprise him even more—that some Republican
senators were willing to stage a filibuster to defeat
his "stimulus package":

THOUGHTS ON FILIBUSTERING

If I were ever called upon to muster
The stamina to mount a filibuster,
I'd start with Army stories—three or four
Of those I guess you had to be there for—
And then I'd bruit about what I could bruit
Of what my kids once said that I found cute.
Then tales of miles per gallon, dental work,
And tales of why the boss is still a jerk.
And as these stories painfully unwound,
I think the other side would come around.

And then the first one hundred days were over and it was time for Clinton's friends in the press to publish their reviews. They did. In fact, there were so many pieces about the first one hundred days that, for a moment there, I start wondering why there was never anything in the paper anymore about Amy Fisher.

ON ATTEMPTING TO COMMENT ON THE FIRST ONE HUNDRED DAYS

"O Muse," I said, "just let me count the ways
Of measuring the first one hundred days—
Of painting, not in blacks or whites but grays,
The complicated story of this phase
Of Clinton's reign: those things that rate
   hoorays

And those things (maybe more) that rate oy
vays.

The muse then said, "I guess you seek to raise
Another crop of journalist clichés.
Why can't you people learn at times it pays
To keep your silence and avert your gaze?
Why can't you see that every reader prays
You'll stop this bunk about a hundred days?"

I said, "I really do respect your views.
I don't intend to argue with a muse."

25. Who's in Charge Here?

I knew very well that it was silly of me to think so, but I couldn't get over the feeling that I might have forced George Stephanopoulos out of his job. This happens to us jackals all the time: we get delusions that we've done some serious damage. At least this time Pete Seeger wasn't involved. Shortly after the first one hundred days, things were not going well at the White House. There was talk about the possibility that the President was gaga over Hollywood people and that his young staff was simply gaga. Suddenly the White House, hinting at serious financial improprieties, replaced its travel staff with some buddies from Little Rock, then called in the FBI to front for a lame attempt to back up the hints, then hired back most of the supposed miscreants:

CHANGES IN TRAVEL PLANS

*The White House canned, and quickly started
    dissing,*
Its travel agents: funds, perhaps, were missing.
And so perhaps were travelers, missent
To places where nobody ever went.
*The World Wide folks from Little Rock had
    come*
To make the White House travel office hum.

The GOP response was swift: "It's sleaze!
These World Wide guys are simply FOBs.
*Complaints against the other folks were
    phonies—*
A way to give the business to some cronies."
*The White House, caught, emitted air and
    foam.*
*Then World Wide booked a one-way ticket
    home.*

The complaints about the travel office had apparently originated with Harry Thomason, Clinton's
television-producer pal, who happened to have an
interest in a company that could have benefited
from the change. Thomason and his wife, Linda
Bloodworth-Thomason—a couple that had already
managed to make us jackals wonder what we found
so objectionable about Bebe Rebozo—staged a me-
dia blitz that seemed to be based on the claim that
they were just folks, and also so rich that White

House travel-office graft would be potatoes too small to be worth their attention.

Thomason expressed shock that White House reporters had asked more questions about the travel-office mess than about some important issues of national security. I tried to explain to him that there was nothing surprising about the reporters' interest in how the White House handled the travel-office episode: they have a perfectly natural human curiosity about how anyone could have done anything that stupid.

There is never any shortage of accounts that detail the historically significant decisions involving war and peace—the Cuban missile crisis, for instance, or the plotting of military strategy in the Gulf War. What is lacking—and what would be infinitely more interesting—is the detailed history of how supposedly shrewd and well-informed people decided to do something truly goofy. How, for instance, had the Nixon Administration reached the decision to outfit the White House guards in uniforms that looked like the work of the only costume designer ever asked to leave a Bavarian opera company because of excess? Did it start one evening when Haldeman said to Ehrlichman, "Do you find yourself moved by the music of Rudolf Friml?" How had Jimmy Carter's staff reached the conclusion that it might be helpful for the President to report that he had been frightened by a rabbit? Was my behind-the-scenes account even close to how George Bush decided that he could jump-start the economy by purchasing four pairs of white athletic socks?

And—to get to the goofball move that followed the travel-office mess by a matter of days—how could a presidential staff let a supposed populist from Arkansas risk even the appearance of tying up traffic at Los Angeles International Airport while he got a two-hundred-dollar haircut from a barber who calls himself Christophe of Beverly Hills? Did anyone think that François Mitterrand, the Socialist President of France, would tie up Orly in order to have his hair trimmed by Tab of Cap d'Antibes or Scott of St.-Tropez?

The only scenario I could come up with, I'm afraid, pointed a finger at George Stephanopoulos, the boy communications director. Stephanopoulos, I speculated, could have acquired a profound belief in the efficacy of hair styling. If not, why would he spend an hour every day training a single lock of hair to fall carelessly toward his boyish brow? Stephanopoulos may have figured it this way: his predecessor, Marlin Fitzwater, was lacking such a lock —as well as a number of other locks—and look what happened to him.

As I envisioned it, the staff meets to decide what President Clinton should do after completing his business—if that's the word—in Los Angeles. Go back to Washington and try to figure out something to do in Bosnia? Stop in the Midwest to rally support for his economic program? Stephanopoulos shakes his head vigorously—a movement that somehow has no effect on the carelessly falling lock. He picks up the telephone. "Get me Christophe of Beverly Hills," he says.

Feeling guilty, I avoided the subject of haircuts when I commented on Stephanopoulos's replacement as White House communications director by David Gergen:

Young Stephanopoulos was very bright.
On multiplicities of facts he'd bone up.
But then the President said, "All and all,
I think, perhaps, we'd better have a grownup."

It may be only coincidental that Marlin Fitzwater, asked that very week about how he'd improve the Clinton White House, said, "A few more fat old bald men wouldn't hurt the place."

26. Another Summer

HOLLYWOOD GOES TOO FAR

Sure, Hollywood is noted for
Its schlocky work. We all get sore
At plots with holes we can't ignore
(About the size of Labrador).
They treat the subject of amour
With lame clichés and schmaltzy score.
They've tried to make us think that war
Is Sly Stallone and gore galore.
Could they do more that I deplore?
Yes, this is worse than heretofore:
They made a creature I adore—
The dinosaur—into a bore.

Yes, it was summer again—the even-dumber season for movies. My wife and I were driving north,
although without hope of escape; we were perfectly

aware that the promotional dinosaur, unlike the real article, has an unlimited range. We were about to brighten up the journey by listening to a cassette of *Molly Ivins Can't Say That, Can She?* Looking over the blurb on the cassette box, my wife read a passage from the tape out loud: "Reagan spent a half hour with the Lebanese Foreign Minister, who was trying to explain the intricate relations between the many political factions in his country. Suddenly Reagan said, 'You know, your nose looks just like Danny Thomas's.' "

I had forgotten about that meeting. It occurred to me that there was something rather comforting about the thought that the country bumbles along ineptly in foreign relations whether the President is a Rhodes Scholar who can rattle off the major mineral resources of Zaire or an old movie actor who may have mistaken the President of France for a delegation of Midwestern turkey farmers. Then a cloud crossed my thoughts.

"Whatever happened to Lebanon?" I asked my wife.

There was a time when you could hear a dozen MLs a week about the brutal, apparently insoluble conflict among those warring factions in Lebanon. But the Danny Thomas anecdote made me realize that I hadn't thought about Lebanon in months.

"And how about Cyprus?" I added. "Whatever happened to Cyprus? How come we don't hear about Cyprus anymore? For that matter, whatever

happened to Northern Ireland? Everything hunky-
dory over there these days?"

WHATEVER HAPPENED TO CYPRUS?

So whatever happened to Cyprus?
So what's with the Turks and the Greeks?
And India? Could Hindus and Muslims
And Sikhs have been peaceful for weeks?
And Lebanon's not in the news now,
Those stories of Lebanon's doom
Are gone from the papers so long I've
Forgotten just who's fighting whom.
And grim talk of Belfast has faded,
Though efforts are made to revive it.
Are all these folks getting along now,
Or killing each other in private?

Someday, I think, we might look back on the
summer of 1993 not as the summer of the dinosaur
but as the time when Bill Clinton began to sound
a little more like George Bush. I don't mean that
he began to sound like someone from Arkansas who
is trying to sound like someone from Connecticut
who is trying to sound like someone from Texas. I
mean that Bill Clinton, with a lot of splashing and
some moments when he seemed in danger of sink-
ing, moved toward the middle of the mainstream.
I suppose that shouldn't have surprised anyone:
American Presidents traditionally move toward the

center, and both Bush and Clinton claimed to be in the center to begin with.

Some people saw a move toward the center in Clinton's decision about who would be nominated to the Supreme Court after Byron White announced his resignation. ("We'll bid adieu to Justice Whizzer White, / A running back who moved well to his right.") After a long search process that showed some signs of having been subcontracted to the Marx Brothers, Clinton named Ruth Bader Ginsburg, a respected moderate who, as a judge on the Circuit Court of Appeals, had often voted with the Reagan-Bush appointees. I did point out that one item on her résumé might have been hard for George Bush to swallow:

ON THE NOMINATION OF
RUTH BADER GINSBURG

She's highly thought of in the trade.
The taxes for her maid were paid.
And somehow all the White House vetters
Remained unmoved by those four letters
That spooked Dukakis through and through—
The dread quartet, ACLU.
The paths in gender law she plowed
Were plowed while working for this crowd.
Republicans don't seem annoyed
To hear the judge was thus employed.
They cheer: She made some law impartial,
And got compared to Thurgood Marshall.

Dukakis, Bush said, had a card—
With that alone poor Mike was tarred.
If Bush's views remain unvarying,
He wonders: Was the judge card-carrying?

When historians are sorting through all this, I suspect they will date the most obvious lurch toward the middle of the road sometime in the near post-haircut period. The haircut and the travel-office mess had made the White House staff look like yahoos. The stimulus package had been defeated, and the rest of Clinton's economic program was bogged down in a Congress controlled by his own party. Clinton's talk concerning what he intended to do about Bosnia had turned out to be air of roughly the same temperature as the talk we were hearing from other world leaders concerning what they intended to do about Bosnia. Clinton's nominee to run the Civil Rights Division of the Justice Department—his old friend Lani Guinier—was being depicted as a radical. Opponents of dropping the ban on gays in the military were sounding adamant. Within a few days, Guinier was out, David Gergen was in, and I could imagine Bill Clinton, in a darkened room late at night, pickin' on his guitar:

BLUES, BY WANDERIN'
WILLIE CLINTON

I got the movin' to the middle 'cause it's slip'ry
*   on the edges blues.*
I gotta clear with the suits every fresh nominee
*   I choose.*
It's a shame about Lani Guinier.
I don't mean to sound insincere,
But I wish she would just disappear.
'Cause she don't represent what I think, at
*   least now, are my views.*
I got the movin' to the middle 'cause it's slip'ry
*   on the edges blues.*

I got the movin' to the middle 'cause it's slip'ry
*   on the edges blues.*
I gotta go with Sam Nunn on the gays, 'cause
*   we don't want no coups.*
He likes that "don't-ask-and-don't-tell."
It ought to serve all those folks well.
If it don't, well, guys, what the hell . . .
'Cause this is a fight that I sure as shootin'
*   would lose.*
I got the movin' to the middle 'cause it's slip'ry
*   on the edges blues.*

By the time Clinton made enough changes in his
economic bill to get it passed, some commentators
were saying that his plan to reduce the deficit
looked an awful lot like Bush's plan to reduce the

deficit. While the bill seemed stalled, Clinton had even been heard to refer to his difficulties with Congress as "the gridlock thing." He had so much in common with Bush, you half expected him to bomb Iraq. And then he bombed Iraq—in retaliation, he said, for the Iraqi plot to assassinate former President George Bush. Some things never change.

SADDAM HUSSEIN, SADDAM HUSSEIN

Saddam Hussein, Saddam Hussein,
Upon whose head our missiles rain,
It's often said that you're a stain,
And maybe just a tad insane
(You seem to think you're Charlemagne),
And therefore we should not refrain
From bombing part of your domain
Until it looks like beef chow mein.

And yet there is a question whether
We'd really like to send you nether.

When diplomatic talk turns plain,
It's said there's value in your reign.
You stabilize and you contain.
You keep some folks from raising cain.
And we use you to show the pain
That those who challenge us obtain—
As you use us when under strain:
We're blamed for what you can't explain.

Although we're birds of different feather,
We may be in this thing together.

All of this was done at a terrific pace. Clinton
treated the presidency as if it were one of those
tour de force acting roles in which the actor is never
offstage. Even in selecting a summer vacation spot
for the President, the Administration seemed to
follow the same pattern it had established in search-
ing for nominees to important positions; there were
even leaks that turned out to be wrong about which
place had it in the bag. Finally, the President chose
Martha's Vineyard, and my colleagues wrote reams
of copy about which local celebrities would be invited to which presidential party. I had written
about Martha's Vineyard myself a couple of times.
I'd referred to it as "the single most difficult place
on the Atlantic Coast for a non-property owner to
get to the beach"—a place where renowned writers
and academics and entertainers of a progressive
bent are given the quiet and leisure they need to
compose NO TRESPASSING signs. In other words,
it seemed at first glance to be an excellent place for
a populist President—most of the celebrities voted
Democratic—but it was, when you came down to
who controlled the real estate and who was kept off
it, not far from a George Bush sort of place. I didn't
air those observations. I was too relieved that, after
what seemed to be an almost endless first act of Bill
Clinton's *tour de force*, we were going to be blessed
with an intermission:

JUST COOL IT

*I liked the way that Reagan simply vanished
 when he could.
For weeks we'd hear a single phrase: "He's
 happy chopping wood."
If we were not aware of him, he didn't seem to
 care.
When Ronald Reagan wasn't there, he simply
 wasn't there.
The bully pulpit stood unmanned. The White
 House was a tomb.
Of course, he sometimes wasn't there when he
 was in the room.*

*This Clinton's with us day and night—his
 voice, his plans, his sax.
At times you want to say, "Hey, Bill, just cool
 it, guy. Relax."
Yes, Clinton needs a rest, all right, and we
 need one from him.
We needn't know with whom he golfs, with
 whom he takes a swim.
We can't absorb so much of him. That's one of
 our frustrations.
I think that our relationship needs separate
 vacations.*

27. *Still Busy, or Busy Again*

No sooner had President Clinton returned to Washington than he seemed busier than ever. His plans for the fall included winning congressional approval for a trade agreement that would transform forever this country's economic relationship with the countries that adjoin it, introducing a plan that would provide the first universal health coverage in American history, and, almost as a sideline, "reinventing government." Next to all that, the earlier activity that had included plans for an American challenge to the airbus and for a change in the way meat is inspected seemed to border on the lethargic.

The point man for the plan to reinvent government was Al Gore, who, according to the sages in Washington, was bouncing back—if that phrase could be applied to someone who was stiff enough to give the impression that one good bounce would

crack him in half. During the transition, as Gore
seemed to settle into the role of the only piece of
chain-saw sculpture in the country with Secret Service protection, there had been some concern that
he might replace Dan Quayle in more ways than
one. Vice Presidents tend to strike people as funny.
The contrast between what a Vice President is officially called on to do (practically nothing) and what
he might have to do (become President) is a source
of uneasy laughter. Vice Presidents, of course,
dream of being President. In their heart of hearts,
they may even dream of suddenly replacing the man
to whom they traditionally display an almost slavish
loyalty—which adds to their comic aspect, since
they are assumed to be in the position of an ever
so polite manservant who makes the hex sign when
his master's back is turned.

By the time Gore started spreading the gospel of
a reinvented government, he had taken steps to
break out of the buffoon mold that can harden
around any Vice President. He was, for instance,
using the prevailing banana peel against himself—
making his own jokes on *The David Letterman
Show* about how wooden he is. Here Gore had an
advantage over Dan Quayle: somehow, telling self-
deprecating jokes about how dumb you are doesn't
quite do the trick.

GORE REDUX

Vice President? The job has been a joke,
Unless the President decides to croak.
When Clinton met the press, young Albert
  Gore
Appeared at first as part of the decor—
An ornament you see upon a hood,
A loyal beast of burden carved of wood.
It was assumed, from Veeps we've had before,
That Clinton was a man whose ox was Gore.

But Gore has broken free of these cruel yokes,
And stand-up comics now refrain from jokes
On how he's formed of stuff that can't be
  dented.
He's now got government all reinvented.
On Letterman *we've seen him do a riff*
On how he manages to be so stiff.
So someday he himself may take the throne,
And try to find an ox all of his own.

As busy as Bill Clinton kept himself, it appeared
that his greatest photo opportunity of the autumn
—maybe of his entire presidency—was to come
about through events that were not of his making.
From all appearances, prospects for peace in the
Middle East were about as dim in the fall of 1993
as they had been for the preceding four decades.
The peace talks seemed to be going nowhere. Yasir
Arafat had managed to cut off his financial arm by

backing Saddam Hussein against the oil states of the Gulf—in terms of long-term financial planning, it was the equivalent of a senator from the state of Washington championing the McDonnell Douglas design over the one submitted by Boeing—and he seemed more and more to be a fading transitional figure, soon to be supplanted by fundamentalist loonies who made him appear almost avuncular. As it turned out, though, representatives of Israel and the PLO had been brought together secretly in Norway, almost by accident, and they were said to have reached an agreement on the first steps toward peace.

A CHEER, OF SORTS, FOR ARAFAT

A cheer, of sorts, for Arafat!
His clever schemes ofttimes fell flat.
Told often by his hosts to scat,
And chased toward corners, like a rat,
Confused about where he was at,
And often wrestled to the mat,
This diplomatic acrobat
Has never landed with a splat.
He rose again, this wily cat,
And now he'll have a habitat—
With time to shave, and change his hat.

Within a couple of weeks, it was agreed that Arafat and Israeli Prime Minister Yitzhak Rabin, a former general who had begun fighting Arabs in

1948, would sign the accord on the lawn of the White House, with Bill Clinton presiding. The question raised again and again was whether or not the two old adversaries would shake hands:

The President that day was smooth as silk.
Rabin and Arafat had looked unbudging.
But then at last they shook each other's hand—
Maneuvered there by Clinton's subtle nudging.

His presidency still cannot be judged.
Historians will surely do that later.
But one thing we can safely venture now:
The man would make a very good headwaiter.

Naturally, former Presidents were invited to the ceremony. The next day three of them—George Bush, Jimmy Carter, and Gerald Ford—held a news conference with Clinton to say that they all supported not only the Middle East accord but also the North American Free Trade Agreement.

ON A FOUR-PRESIDENT PRESS
CONFERENCE

The picture lingers in my mind.
I really didn't expect to find
These Presidents all in accord—
Not Clinton, Carter, Bush, and Ford.

About the flag and motherhood
They don't agree—or never could—
On if the flag can be defiled,
Or if she has to have the child.

With NAFTA, disagreement ceases:
All bet it makes us rich as Croesus.
Unanimous, they seek to serve us.
So why does this make people nervous?

28. Another Autumn

THE PHILLIES VS. TORONTO

Toronto is a snappy team—all svelte,
No overgut that covers up the belt.
The Phillies? Ah, that rinky-dink brigade:
Resembling a bed that's left unmade,
They look as if they'd find a grate palatial.
Their hair's a tangled mess—that's head and
   facial.
They chew large wads of gum and gunk.
   What's more,
The stuff they spit will eat away the floor.
The Phillies are the answer to my dream:
Who would have thought that slobs could have
   a team?
They won their league. They almost won it all,
Despite their flab, their high cholesterol.

Toronto won. How sad! For this amounts
To evidence that neatness really counts.

Traditionally, the serious political campaign season gets started as soon as the World Series is over.
Actually, 1993 was an election year for only a few
of the offices that are watched closely by the sort
of commentator whose task it is to explain to voters
what they actually meant by their votes. Governors
were to be elected in Virginia and New Jersey; New
York City would elect a mayor. Perhaps because
the jackals of the press were deprived of their preferred ration of autumn politics, they treated Bill
Clinton's efforts on behalf of the North American
Free Trade Agreement and the Clinton health plan
as political campaigns. So did Clinton. He gave a
rousing speech to Congress to introduce the Administration's health plan—a plan that had emerged
from months of work led by Hillary Rodham Clinton
and Ira Magaziner, one of the President's heavy-
thinking pals from Oxford days—and then stumped
the country on its behalf as if he were seventy-two
hours from Election Day. Harnessing the public
concern about health care that had become obvious
in Harris Wofford's campaign two years before, the
Clinton Administration seemed to have established
as a given for the first time that all Americans would
be covered by some form of health insurance. But
the plan it presented to Congress, supposedly designed to save money by streamlining, struck some

people as an unwieldy beast that might be difficult
to pay for:

A HEALTH CARE PLAN IS SENT
TO CONGRESS

Could anyone be keener
Than Ira Magaziner?
He is the moment's man.
According to his plan,
If you see turvy-topsy
Or suffer from the dropsy,
A doctor will be there.
That's universal care.
And we'll help pay for that
By slicing off the fat
Of bureaucratic forms
And bureaucrats in swarms.
Red tape will disappear.
A bill, precise and clear,
Assures this for the ages.
It's thirteen hundred pages.

But just as Bush's efforts to put the world in order
had been interrupted all the time by domestic problems that his staff decided simply had to be brought
to his attention ("Terribly sorry to disturb you, Mr.
President. It's about this recession . . ."), Clinton
found his concentration on domestic issues dis-
turbed by questions about, say, why our troops
were not in Bosnia or why they *were* in Somalia.

Questions about the latter intensified when, after a disastrous firefight in Mogadishu, the body of an American soldier was dragged through the streets and an American helicopter pilot was held hostage for several days. There were speeches in Congress demanding that the United States pull out of Somalia immediately:

ON MILITARY INTERVENTION

When superpower duty calls abroad,
It's easy sending soldiers into action:
The country stands as one behind our boys.
The problems come arranging their extraction.

Some soldiers pay the price, and Congress
*   howls:*
"This operation is a mess. We must depart."
By then it's hard to find a pol who can
Recall that he was for it at the start.

Of course, any number of reasons, military and political, could be offered to explain why the United States had chosen to intervene in Somalia and not in Bosnia. I suspect, though, that a reasonably detached alien from another planet would emerge from a study of American foreign policy in the past half century with an explanation that is not often heard from American earthlings: names in the former Yugoslavia being notoriously difficult to pronounce, that conflict lacked the two-syllable villain around whom Americans prefer to personalize a crusade: Hitler, Tojo, Stalin, Castro, Saddam. Somalia, on the other hand, had such a figure—a man with a two-syllable name that was not only pronounceable but eminently rhymable:

WHO?

Who was it we once treated as a man to
heed—
A chap who said America should intercede
Because there were Somalis whom we had to
feed?
Aidid.
Whose capture for his villainy have we
decreed,
With thoughts that U.S. Rangers soon would
have him treed
Or helicopter gunships have him fricasseed?
Aidid.
Who is the man we like now that our guy's
been freed—
The man who might become the ruler that we
need
To talk to now and then, the guy we can't
misread?
It isn't André Gide.
It can't be Donna Reed.
Aidid.

There was more unwelcome news for Clinton in November, when the Republicans won all three of the nationally spotlighted elections. Naturally, the Republicans said that the results reflected voter displeasure with Bill Cinton, and the Democrats said that the results reflected only local issues. (When Tip O'Neill said, "All politics is local," he might have added, "All alibis is also local.") The bloom was taken off one of the victories when Ed Rollins, who had managed the successful gubernatorial campaign of Christine Todd Whitman in New Jersey, told a group of reporters that one of the secrets of its success was using $500,000 to encourage black voters to stay home—a confession he soon recanted.

ED ROLLINS SPEAKS

Once Florio had offered his concession,
Ed Rollins made a campaign pro's confession:
We clever dogs, he said, did some suppression
Of votes that could express the wrong
    expression.
If braggadocio is Ed's obsession,
That might, they said, explain this indiscretion.
Still, Ed's career is due for repossession.

Presumably Clinton went through the campaign season trying to keep partisan comments to a minimum: with organized labor bitterly opposed to the North American Free Trade Agreement, its chances of being passed by the House of Representatives depended on enormous support from the Republican side. After a slow start, Clinton had decided to go all-out to win passage of NAFTA. As the day of the House vote approached with the pro-NAFTA forces in the House trailing, many political commentators said that Bill Clinton would lose the battle—and with it any chance he might have had to conduct an effective presidency. Of course, predictions that the presidency of this promising young man would soon lie in ruins had been in the air almost from the day he took office.

CLINTON REDUX

They thought he'd be, with all his smarts,
A master of the presidential arts.
But did he have the stuff that leaders need?
With military gays, Guinier, Aidid,
He seemed not sure precisely what to do.
Supporters groaned. The press declared him
*   through.*
But when it came to NAFTA—Bush's plan—
He deftly gathered up the ball and ran.
He swiveled down the field to great hurrahs,
And stiff-armed labor's leaders in the schnozz.
When his side balked, he got the GOP,
And now the doubters know what he can be
(A role appropriate for such a smarty):
The leader of the opposition party.

Clinton's triumph—amassing Republican votes to assure the passage of an agreement the Republicans had negotiated—was, in fact, a reminder that the office a President holds may be more central to his actions than the party he belongs to. The presence of American troops in Somalia also represented a decision by Bush, between Clinton's election and his inauguration, but Clinton had supported the decision: in general, it's the role of the President to send troops and the role of the Congress to complain that they've been there too long. The sight of those four Presidents standing in the White House together to support NAFTA had reminded me that Presidents of the United States tend to blend together into a tallish white Christian male called Mr. President, who dresses conservatively and shakes hands a lot and habitually reflects both mild irritation with the press and some level of discomfort with Congress. At the Middle East ceremony, a staff member who referred to George Bush as "the President" was corrected by Bush himself ("ex, ex, ex, ex"). Was it possible, I wondered, that people were having trouble telling him from Bill Clinton? Were their Administrations also blending together? As some of the young tigers left over from Clinton's campaign had faded into the background, that first impression of a White House being run by a particularly intense gaggle of wonky graduate students had passed. I began to notice a lot of men in suits. One of them, David Gergen, looked awfully familiar. It occurred to me that the name of the Secretary of Agriculture had slipped my mind.

I saw myself back in that saloon frequented by the small-joke jackals of the press. The atmosphere is glum.

"When it comes to truly colorful characters," Dave is saying, "I've been wondering how Warren Christopher would compare to, say, the leading undertaker of Eau Claire, Wisconsin, or a vice president of the South Central Association of Actuaries."

"Has anybody noticed how much Mack McClarty looks like Samuel Skinner?" Art asks.

"Regular features!" Doug, the political cartoonist, says. "Jesus, I hate regular features!"

"We are sculptors without clay," Russell says.

"Cheer up, guys," the bartender says as he hands around fresh beers. "At least you've got Al Gore."

The response is a line of poisonous looks, because we don't have Al Gore. Al Gore is making his own Al Gore jokes on *Letterman*; Al Gore is pulverizing Ross Perot on *Larry King*. I know things will probably get better for us. Maybe an indictment will come along, or at least a particularly embarrassing scandal. I know we're a long way from an Administration painted in the color we now know as Bush gray. Still, just for that moment, I catch myself thinking, Where are you, Sununu, now that we need you?

29. My Life as a Doggerelist

I'm at my desk—not waiting for a muse
But for the Times, the Post, the Daily News.
For deadline poets, muses are much rarer
Than tuning in MacNeil and his friend Lehrer.
It's they who, perched like ravens on my sill,
Deposit grist that's needed for my mill.*
I'm stuck. I'm blank. The dreaded deadline looms.
I feel my brain is suited for legumes.
I cruise around the dial, I turn the page
To see who might appear upon the stage
As players whom their countrymen salute,
And targets for my bag of rotten fruit.

The news presents a motley little band
That I observe, tomato in my hand:

* Though I'm not up to sonnets or haiku,
  I thought at least one metaphor was due.

The congressmen fine-tuned to every fax
That indicates the wishes of their PACs;
The White House staff, the President's defenders,
All working late, and all in their suspenders;
The tasseled lobbyists, may God forgive us,
Who entertain with steaks washed down with
   Chivas;
A President who always makes me feel
The last one was attacked with too much zeal;
A candidate who poses as our savior.

It helps if all are on their worst behavior.
The job of deadline poet is a calling
Dependent always on the most appalling
Behavior that our public figures show—
Supplies of which seem rarely to run low.
Rascality is what we need, plus greed
Overt enough to draw a blush from Tweed.
A fool is fine. A pompous fool's sublime.
It also helps if they have names that rhyme.